THE AMERICAN VISION

LANDSCAPE PAINTINGS
OF THE
UNITED STATES

THE AMERICAN VISION

LANDSCAPE PAINTINGS
OF THE
UNITED STATES

by Malcolm Robinson

PORTLAND HOUSE
New York

Editor: Marilyn Inglis
Editorial Consultant: Andrew Heritage
Art Editor: David Rowley
Designer: Simon Loxley
Picture Researcher: Kathy Lockley
Production Controller: Garry Lewis

First published in Great Britain in 1988 by
Octopus Books Limited,
Michelin House,
81 Fulham Road, London SW3 6RB

This 1988 edition published by Portland House,
a division of dilithium Press Ltd
Distributed by Crown Publishers, Inc.,
225 Park Avenue South,
New York, New York   10003

Printed and bound by Mandarin Offset in Hong Kong

ISBN 0-517-66191-8
h g f e d c b a

For Alice Ruby Robinson
and the late John Walker Robinson

Jacket illustration: Cranberry Pickers (c.1870–80)
by Eastman Johnson (Yale University Art Gallery).
Title page: Cliffs of the Upper Colorado River,
Wyoming Territory (1882) by Thomas Moran (National
Museum of American Art, Smithsonian Institution).

CONTENTS

FOREWORD

The landscape paintings of the United States are seen in this book against the backdrop of political and social events – the Declaration of Independence, the drive west, the Civil War and the turmoil of the twentieth century, with its two World Wars and its Great Depression. The growth of means of communication over this period was of paramount significance; they cover the horse-drawn vehicles of the eighteenth and nineteenth centuries, the spread of the railroad in the nineteenth century and the incredible technological developments of the twentieth century.

The landscapes of the time documented many of the results of these developments but also developed many ideas independent of them; American

*T*his early American landscape represents a first essential step in the development of the American Dream. Known principally as a portraitist, and ironically forced to flee the newly-independent nation in 1777 (he supported the losing side), Earl returned to a successful career in New York and Connecticut after 1785.

This version of the American landscape is very much the New English one, not only in its geographical setting but also in an abstract political sense. The wilderness might never have existed. The landscape of gently rolling dales is tamed and tilled, dotted with villages – it is the America which Britain fought hard to retain, an extension of the old country's own mythic Merrie England.

And this of course is precisely what many of the earliest settlers had labored long to achieve, a home away from home, a land with all the familiar trappings of their birthplace, but free from the political and ideological mores which blighted England and much of Europe. Earl's vision captures this, but offers no hint of the great promise and challenge which galvanized the young nation in the nineteenth century □

landscape painting is not merely an art of reportage. The peace of the mid-nineteenth century, for example, enabled a group of American artists to develop a landscape style of their own which found expression in the accomplishments of the Hudson River School.

The art of every nation is the result of a series of influences, and that of the United States is no exception to this. In the twentieth century, with its rapid worldwide communication, national barriers to the arts have disappeared and developments in Europe are seen and adapted in the United States just as quickly as American ideas make their impact on European art, resulting in a greater interchange of influences than ever before.

Ralph Earl
Looking East From Denny Hill 1800
45¾″ × 79⅜″
Worcester Art Museum, Massachusetts

AN EMERGING NATION

It would be convenient for art historians if all major national, political and social upheavals were reflected in the art of that country. For example, one can cite the rise of neo-classicism in France which echoed the republican virtues of the revolutionary period; or the negative impact on the arts in Germany of the rise of the National Socialist party and the consequent closing of the Bauhaus in the 1930s; or the influence on both Western and Oriental art by the opening of Japan by Commodore Perry in the nineteenth century. However, the continuity of American art was scarcely disturbed by the Revolution in 1776. Although leading intellectuals expressed a need for a native American art at this stage the achievement of such a thing would have to wait for many years.

Thomas Jefferson and his contemporaries saw a parallel between their age and that of classical antiquity and the classical revival which was spreading through Europe in the work of such artists as Jacques Louis David, replacing the frivolity of the Rococo style. Although the architecture of the early republican period in America followed these neo-classic forms, the painters of this period seemed unaware of these theories and the artistic traditions of England continued to be the primary source of style in America until well after the turn of the century.

The strong feeling of national pride following the American Revolution produced a demand for portraits of American heroes, but the styles and characteristics that persisted were those established in the Colonial period – a style based on the English portrait tradition brought to America by immigrant artists such as John Smibert, a Scotsman trained in the English tradition of Sir Godfrey Kneller. The backgrounds of these portraits in the eighteenth century were executed as thinly-painted and indistinct backdrops which were not related spatially to the main subject of the painting – the portrait of the sitter. These works were naive and provincial by comparison with English portraiture, a watered-down version imported by lesser artists; the success of these artists was due to the fact that in comparison to the limner tradition their work appeared professional. The limners carried on the seventeenth-century style with its naive vision and limited technique, their bold linear approach and flat pattern producing an unflattering image of their sitter.

The ideas established by Smibert were continued in the next generation of American portrait painters, probably the best of whom was Robert Feke who, though breaking with the stock postures for his sitters, continued the tradition of painted backdrops behind the

John F. Vanderlyn
Niagara Falls from Table Rock 1801–2
24″ × 30″
Courtesy Museum of Fine Arts, Boston

*V*anderlyn's first-hand experience of the European art market, gleaned while working in Paris, opened his eyes to the possibilities of exploiting the lucrative trade in engraved and painted views. Although detailed topographical knowledge of North America was still limited to the area east of the Mississippi basin, the New World offered a wealth of natural splendors, foremost among them being the Niagara Falls which Vanderlyn painted in preparation for a print series. This composition ably conveys the sheer spectacle of the enormous cataract on the Niagara River, and attempts to capture the famous spray clouds bursting at the foot of the cascade. The flattened serpentine of the composition enhances the feeling of scale, as does the inclusion of tiny figures – both sightseers and natives – in the foreground, a particular device of traditional European classical landscapists. The rather sharp tonal contrasts and marked highlights of the breaking water would have been of considerable help to the subsequent monotone engraver □

figures. Portraits were perceived as a visible status symbol in the late eighteenth century and were commissioned by the merchant classes, who were gaining increasing prosperity at the time. Although there is evidence that eighteenth-century painting included works other than portraits, these other forms tended to be more in the style of decorative folk art, either as wall decoration or on overmantels or other household furniture.

The main developments in art at this time were happening in England, with the founding of the Royal Academy in 1769, the genesis of a body of writings on art by such people as its first president, Sir Joshua Reynolds, and the establishment by him of the Grand Style, with its emphasis on the ideal standards of beauty with reference to the antique via the Italian Renaissance. After the Revolution the visual arts were still a luxury in America, with portraiture perceived as the only utilitarian form of art and so the only acceptable one. Any excursions into the realms of landscape were thus by those artists earning their living from portraits. Sir Joshua Reynolds, who prescribed the hierarchy of artistic values in eighteenth-century England, stated that landscape painting ranked below history painting and this lowly opinion of landscape seemed to be accepted in America. Many American artists went to Europe to learn from the Old Masters, particularly from the artists of the Italian High Renaissance, and to absorb the lessons of the Grand Style – described by Reynolds in his *Discourses* as the supreme form of art.

Landscape Painting Emerges

In the late eighteenth and early nineteenth centuries England produced many landscape artists, of whom the most famous were Thomas Gainsborough, Richard Wilson, John Constable and Joseph Mallord William Turner. Many lesser English artists came to America, bringing with them some of their more illustrious compatriots' ideas. Among these artists were Archibald Robertson and his brother Alexander, who established the Columbian Academy of Painting, probably the first art school in New York; William Winstanley, who painted in a style reminiscent of Richard Wilson; and many others, including William Russell Birch and his son Thomas, a topographical painter.

When the American artist Ralph Earl (1751–1801) returned from his studies in England in 1785 he began to produce portraits of a type in which the landscape background was not only important as part of the overall picture but also broke with the previous generalized images and presented instead a specific scene, such as the Connecticut landscape of his *Mrs William Mosely and Her Son Charles* (1791). His first purely landscape painting is *Looking East from Denny Hill*, painted c. 1800, and though compositionally a little naive, with a tree on either side framing a distant view, it is a perceptive forerunner of the Hudson River School.

A popular art form in the eighteenth century was the engraving based on a painting. This had been used successfully in England by William Hogarth in various series such as the *Rake's Progress* and *Marriage à la Mode* and it was a way of making art accessible to the public. John Vanderlyn (1775–1852) took with him to Paris studies of Niagara Falls which he had engraved in England and produced as a print series with the intention of selling them to supplement his income and thus enable him to extend his stay in France. Ralph Earl had already exhibited a view of the Falls in New York and Philadelphia in 1800 with great public response and Vanderlyn's choice of Niagara Falls as a subject for popular prints in Europe was a sound one.

On this first visit to Paris Vanderlyn trained in the French neo-classic manner in the studio of Francis André Vincent, where he absorbed the style of precise draftsmanship and clear modeling. During his second visit to Europe he spent some time in Rome, where he painted *Marius Among the Ruins of Carthage* which gained him the gold medal from Napoleon Bonaparte in the Paris Salon in 1808. On his return to America in 1815 he brought with him sketches of the gardens of Versailles which he transferred to 3,000 square feet (279 square metres) of canvas in a vast panorama, exhibiting this in a custom-built museum in the form of a rotunda in New York.

Panoramas had become popular in England by the 1780s and 1790s. The best of these kept visitors sufficiently far away from the painting to prevent brushstrokes from being distracting and the effect of passing from a dark entrance passage into the fully-lit scene surrounded by a huge painting must have been very impressive. The concept spread

Washington Allston
Moonlit Landscape 1819
24″ × 35″
Courtesy Museum of Fine Arts, Boston

*T*his deceptive canvas gives the impression of being a grand
Romantic gesture on a large scale. In fact the painting itself is
quite small (less than 2 ft by 3 ft) but it contains within it the seeds
of American Romanticism which were to germinate and flower in
the work of the Hudson River School. The foreground contains
details reminiscent of the European landscape tradition – the
beached gaff cutter, the low bridge and the indefinite (possibly
ruined) buildings in the middle ground. However the combination of
mountains and flat plains stretching into a seemingly endless
distance have a fresh feeling – something of the infinite promise of
the American landscape which later fascinated the Hudson River
painters.

Allston has also added something new in the whole ambience of
the composition: bathed in a benevolent but mysterious moonlight a
group of figures enter a strange dialogue, while a solitary figure
makes his way from the riverside. Above them fantastic clouds map
the sky. There is an enigmatic quality to the scene which invites
comparison with the work of the Surrealists a century later, but
which may be more closely dated to the current Gothic vogue, and

indeed Allston himself had attempted to write a Gothic novel. This
painting was executed at a relatively late stage in Allston's career
and foreshadows some of the works of the Luminist School which
appeared several years later □

across the Atlantic, American entrepreneurs importing them from England and extending their potential audience by sending them on tour. The American panorama at this time was ranked with freak shows and waxworks and was not seen as the art form it was in England. It was normally painted by theater set painters and was usually less sophisticated than its English counterpart. Vanderlyn exhibited his *Palace and Gardens of*

The resemblance of this scene to the Flemish and Dutch landscape schools of the sixteenth and seventeenth centuries is no accident. Brooklyn was originally a Dutch settlement (Breuckelen) and although latterly under English control, aspects of that underlying Dutch influence, which marks much of the New York area even today, can be seen in the low-eaved roofs, tall chimneys and lipped roofs of the settlement portrayed here. The attention to the everyday detail of village life and the choice of winter scene of course further the resemblance. But in style this painting represents something quite different; the straightforward uncomplicated style of representation, bordering on the naive in its pragmatism, identifies an enduring and popular strain in American art which rejects the "difficult" or "intellectual" in favor of more honest celebrations of the workaday existence □

Versailles along with other works, thinking of this as a step towards a national art museum, but the inclusion of the nude *Ariadne*, plus Vanderlyn's copies of Titian's *Danae* and Correggio's *Antiope*, disturbed the puritanical American society of the day. Unfortunately Vanderlyn's Versailles panorama was not financially successful. He took it on tour to the South but the novelty of this type of exhibition was wearing off.

Francis Guy
Winter Scene in Brooklyn
c. 1817–20
60″ × 76″
The Brooklyn Museum

*T*he naive element in American landscape painting would continue to remain very close to the surface of the American view of their world. It informed the immensely popular Currier and Ives series of prints of the late nineteenth century and re-emerged as a central force in the Regionalist schools of the twentieth century. At the core of this tradition were the echoes down the years of arts and crafts styles developed by the first settlers. This curious painting, from the mid-nineteenth century, perfectly captures this spirit. The handling of the obstructive mass of the wooded bluff at the center of the painting is reminiscent of decorative patchwork, while the inclusion of the details of the landscape – flowers, trees, boats and buildings – is similar in manner to the style of embroidered samplers. This view is notable however in combining the idyll of the domestic landscape (see page 9) with an admiration for the continuing presence and dominance of the wilderness □

Thomas Chambers
The Connecticut Valley
Mid-nineteenth century
18″ × 24″
National Gallery of Art,
Washington DC

Traveling Art

The interest in art in the Early Republic centered on traveling shows and the panorama painting, but it was an interest in novelty, sensation and amusement rather than in any artistic quality: several of the privately-owned museums of the time showed art alongside natural history displays and the involvement of the famous showman Phineas T. Barnum, who took over the museums run by Peale and Scudder, reinforced this image of the art museum as a sideshow.

The sheer spectacle of Niagara Falls attracted many artists, including John Trumbull (1756–1843), who in 1808 produced two wide horizontal format oil paintings of the Falls. By this time the Falls were a major attraction and Trumbull was the first artist to combine this popular subject with the entertainment format of the panorama. These paintings were executed on a smaller scale than Vanderlyn's Versailles panorama, with the intention of enlarging them for bigger venues. Like Vanderlyn, Trumbull was attempting to bring his work to more people and thus produce more income. In these paintings he followed the traditional classical landscape format of symmetrical coulisses or banks on the right and left of the canvas and placed the Falls in the center. In his *View of the Falls of Niagara from under Table Rock* a group of Indians was included in the left foreground to add the picturesque element which appealed to nineteenth-century taste, particularly in England. Trumbull took these 14-foot (4-metre) paintings to England, intending to produce a large-scale panorama, but he was unable to find backers for the project and so sent them back to America in 1813.

Trumbull's landscape paintings are but a minor part of his output and he is best known as the painter of the Revolution. Following the example of many American artists of the day, in 1784 he studied with Benjamin West in London; he became interested in history painting, but turned away from classical mythology to contemporary events. While in London, he spent his time working on a series of paintings based on the events of the American Revolution. In 1817 he became President of the American Academy in New York and oversaw the direction of American art for the next ten years.

The English Connection

Washington Allston (1779–1843) studied at the Royal Academy under West, who succeeded Sir Joshua Reynolds as its president in 1792. In London Allston met Vanderlyn and together they visited Paris via the Netherlands. The neo-classicism of Paris did not appeal to Allston as it did to Vanderlyn and the former's work began to reflect his studies of the Venetians in the Louvre. After settling in Rome for several years in the company of an international group of artists and writers such as Vanderlyn, Coleridge, Keats, Shelley and Turner, Allston returned to Boston in 1808. Here he painted portraits for a few years and then retraced his steps to England. He returned to the United States in 1818 and painted romantic images, including *Moonlit Landscape* (1819). He had painted landscapes such as *Landscape with a Lake* as early as 1804 but the conviction of the age was that history painting ranked highest in the visual arts and Allston subscribed to this with a series of neo-classic paintings, including *Prophet Jeremiah Dictating to the Scribe Baruch* (1820) which contained echoes of Michelangelesque figures.

Allston saw Michelangelo as a forerunner of the romantic artist and, just as Michelangelo's commission of the tomb of Pope Julius II hung over him for 40 years, so a commissioned work was to dog Allston for a major part of his active life. His *Belshazzar's Feast*, begun in England, was to occupy him for the last 25 years of his life. It was endowed by ten Boston gentlemen and he felt unable to abandon it, despite the changes taking place in his work.

Moonlit Landscape belongs to this late stage of his career and foreshadows some of the Luminist works of the 1850s and 1860s. With its glowing color and strong design, it had some impact on the romantic naturalists of the Hudson River School and this romantic vision opened up new directions in American art. The concern with light in this and many other nineteenth-century landscape paintings heralds the development of Impressionism in France but, unlike Impressionism, it never extended to becoming solely analytical of light. For American artists of this period it was a means of showing their awareness of God and light never becomes separated from the subject represented. In this landscape Allston produced an emotional, lyrical image rather than a record of an event or place and it is this contribution which was to be pursued by later landscape artists as they moved away from their purely topographical studies.

While Allston was concerned with the romantic lyricism of his *Moonlit Landscape*, Francis Guy (1760–1820) was working in the topographical realism which continued in popularity well into the nineteenth century. Born in the Lake District in England, Guy came to America as a tailor and taught himself to paint using a method described by Rembrandt Peale in which the image is drawn in chalk on to black gauze stretched across a frame set up in front of the subject to be reproduced. The drawn image can then be easily transferred to canvas by simple hand pressure. This technique is similar to the

The development of a national school of landscape painting in the young nation was inevitably dogged by the older artistic traditions of Europe. It was only when native artists began to deal with the new landscape about them in a direct fashion, on its own terms as it were, that the beginnings of something new began to clearly emerge.

Alvan Fisher was a provincial artist of considerable natural talent and great compositional judgement; this painting is both mature in style and remains largely undiluted by superficial references to previous European traditions, although it remains basically classical in manner, and shows that Fisher was probably familiar with the German school through engravings. What emerges here is a truly awe-inspiring representation of nature in all her majesty. In this it looks forward to the achievement of the Hudson River School in breaking free from the chains of European tradition and forging a style which could do the American landscape justice □

linear perspective devices invented by Filippo Brunelleschi in the early fifteenth century in Florence. In his work *Winter Scene in Brooklyn*, painted between 1817 and 1820, Guy has rejected any reference to the picturesque or ideal and shows instead a meticulously presented image of a town. He has enhanced what could have been a rather arid, mechanically-produced image with numerous figures going about their everyday occupations to produce a painting reminiscent of Brueghel.

The Hudson River School

The 1820s saw the stirrings of the first national landscape school around the Hudson River, but at the same time other landscapists were working alongside this mainstream

Alvan Fisher
The Great Horseshoe Fall, Niagara 1820
34⅜″ × 48½″
National Museum of American Art, Smithsonian Institution

movement. This work varied in quality a great deal but some fine work was produced by Alvan Fisher, notably *Great Horseshoe Fall, Niagara* (1820). Fisher started as a country store clerk and then took up portrait painting, traveling to Europe in 1825 to study. *Great Horseshoe Fall, Niagara*, though in many ways betraying his provincial origins (particularly in the rendering of the foreground figures and foliage), shows a good grasp of light and space in the well-realized distant landscape and the convincing water, with the rainbow on the left linking the foreground to the clouds sweeping across the landscape.

Although belonging to the same generation as the Hudson River School, Samuel F.B. Morse (1791–1872) produced landscapes very different from theirs. While he studied history painting for four years at the studio of Benjamin West in the company of Washington Allston, on his return to the United States in 1815 he set himself up as a portrait painter in Boston. As a portraitist he produced many fine works including the full-length portrait of *The Marquis de Lafayette* (1826) for New York City but, in spite of his artistic successes, like Trumbull and Vanderlyn he was not financially successful as an artist. He produced several landscapes and in them he avoided the picturesqueness favored by so many of his contemporaries. In its place he portrayed the realism of everyday scenes, much as Francis Guy had in his *Winter Scene in Brooklyn*. Morse's *View from Apple Hill* (c. 1829) shows American women in an American landscape with houses and barns rather than the idylls of nymphs in an Arcadian setting with classical ruins, although the composition owes a debt to the Italian High Renaissance.

Morse's interest in painting was not sustained and by 1837 he had completely abandoned it in favor of his inventions. History remembers him as the creator of the telegraph, while his fame as a painter has diminished.

The concept of reverence for nature untouched by man became a dominant theme in the nineteenth century and it was this sentiment that led to the popularity and progression of landscape painting in this period. It was a time when the grandeur of the American scenery attracted tourists, while artists depicted it as a means of emphasizing its religious or philosophic connections.

Dates marking the beginning, or indeed the end, of art movements are difficult to determine and often arbitrary. However, 1825 is important in relation to the beginning of the Hudson River School for it was in this year that Thomas Cole (1801–1848) was 'discovered' by three leading New York artists, John Trumbull, Asher B. Durand and William Dunlap.

**Thomas Cole
The Oxbow (The Connecticut River near Northampton)** 1836
51½″ × 76″
The Metropolitan Museum of Art

**Samuel F. B. Morse
View of Apple Hill** c. 1829
22″ × 29″
Private Collection

*T*he notion of America as the realization of an Arcadian idyll was another European idea naturally favored by classicists and historicists alike, and which was difficult for Americans to shake off. After all, Jefferson himself had set about giving the new republic a classical image. Samuel F. B. Morse established an interesting compromise by deploying the classical manner and ambience while replacing certain essential elements with a more realistic view of his subject. Here a traditional classical scheme of receding and advancing planes, with a distinctly Renaissance foreground figure group, is played off against a particularly unpicturesque bridge, the stark qualities of some (possibly industrial) frame barns, and rising from the wooded slopes in the distance, a tall smoking chimney. The even lighting scheme, too, is unusually devoid of theatrical effects. In sum, the painting (like Morse's own career as both a painter and inventor) embodies the twin aspirations of the first generation of independent Americans – the yearning for cultural tradition while readily embracing the fresh and the new.

Thomas Cole was undoubtedly the finest painter of the Hudson River School. Although the underlying influence of the European tradition of Classical and Romantic landscape painting heavily informed his work, his greatest inspiration was clearly provided by the scale, splendor and diversity of the New World landscape. A measure of his achievement is that, by the mid-1830s, the subject of his landscape paintings could not be mistaken for any other part of the world. He previously acknowledged this debt; 'the painter of American scenery has, indeed, privileges superior to any other; all Nature here is new to Art'. In this statement he clearly identified that feature which makes his work so distinctive, for despite the fundamentally traditional formula of his style, Cole's approach to the American landscape was completely fresh, relied on conveying surprise and awe by dramatic exaggerations of scale and form □

The Hudson River School is a misleading term, since it was neither a school with a unified style nor did all its artists live in one area. They did, however, all share similar ideas about romantic landscapes and believed that the scenery of the United States was more beautiful than that of any other country. They held the view that a landscape in its virgin state, unsullied by the inroads of civilization, was closer to God.

Thomas Cole was born in Lancashire, England, in 1801. In 1818 he came with his parents to America, where he worked as an engraver, art teacher, designer and general handyman before turning his efforts fully to painting. In 1825, when Trumbull, Durand and Dunlap bought three landscapes of Cole's in New York, they introduced him to a literary circle which included the poet William Cullen Bryant. Just as Washington Allston found strong links with major literary figures in England and America, so Cole and Bryant found similar points of contact in their work, in particular in their response to nature. The friendship of these two men was commemorated in Asher B. Durand's painting *Kindred Spirits*, showing them on a rocky ledge overlooking a landscape.

After his recognition by Trumbull and his companions Cole was established in New York and spent much of his time on sketching tours up the Hudson valley gathering information for his paintings. Although landscape was the source of their work the majority of artists at this time still produced their paintings in the studio from sketches and Cole was no exception to this. In these early works he created a formula of dramatic foregrounds with an elevated distant vista.

In 1829 Cole traveled to England, France and Italy, where he was attracted to the work of Turner, Richard Wilson, Claude Lorraine and Salvator Rosa. After his journeys his work showed a new monumentality and a concern with romantic ideas. The influence of Turner's *Building of Carthage* is seen in a series of five canvases depicting the *Course of Empire* painted between 1833 and 1836 for Luman Reed, an important patron of American art in New York. Many of his works from this period show Cole's preoccupation with the theme of death which is typical of the sentiments of the age. Contemporaneously with the end of this series Cole produced one of his greatest landscape paintings – *The Oxbow*, which he called *View from Mount Holyoake after a Thunderstorm*, a topographically accurate representation of an immense vista of the Connecticut River valley. In this he abandons the literary romantic references that appear in such paintings as his *Course of Empire, Departure, Return,* and *Voyage of Life* but he has imbued it with a romantic sensibility in the gnarled and twisted tree trunks on the left, a device adopted from Italianate painters such as Richard Wilson. This device probably has its origin in the work of Salvator Rosa and it features in many romantic landscapes of the nineteenth century, appearing in Cole's work as late as 1846 in *The Mountain Ford*. With this Cole combines a passing storm at the upper left just as Alvan Fisher did in his *Great Horseshoe Fall, Niagara* of 1820.

Cole's concern with observation and the expression of lofty ideals became the mainstay of American landscapes in the mid-nineteenth century. In spite of his belief in the inclusion of great detail in his landscapes, he always allowed time to elapse between his studies and the finished painting. This idea of permitting time to act as a filter of unessential elements is echoed in the writings of William Wordsworth, who favored 'images recollected in tranquility'.

William Cullen Bryant's sentiments in *Thanatopsis* that the physical world is a manifestation of God finds a parallel in Cole's landscapes – for example *The Oxbow*, with its sense of change, of calm and storm, of life in the growing tree and death in the shattered and twisted trunk. This was the first of the series of major works extolling the virtues of American scenery. Cole's romanticism is evident in his attachment to the image of the wilderness. Although the nineteenth century was a time of intrusion by the railroad into the countryside Cole produced paintings which ignored this encroachment, even in the instance of the Catskill and Canajoharie Railroad moving near to his own land. His *View on the Catskill, Early Autumn* (1837) ignored this development, retaining the unpolluted image of the wilderness, and it was another six years before he included the presence of the railroad tracks in a painting.

The artist who is often considered the co-founder of the Hudson River School, although he did not work in the Hudson River area until late in life, is Thomas Doughty (1793–

Thomas Doughty
A River Glimpse 1890
30¼″ × 25″
The Metropolitan Museum
of Art

*T*homas Doughty ranks among the leading exponents of the
English Romantic landscape school in America. The influence
of Constable is clear in his free handling of paint and his
instinctive, almost improvised methods of manipulation of color,
color contrasts and highlights – all of which point to his intense
observation of nature. Although such a canvas as this would not
have been painted en plein air, it is undoubtedly the result of a
large number of careful color sketches and studies. The result,
however, retains a freshness absent from the more calculated and
dramatic effects achieved by Thomas Cole, and it is interesting to

note that Doughty was largely self-taught.

Doughty, although normally associated closely with the Hudson
River School, did not indulge in their more typical eulogies to
nature, preferring rather to present nature on a more intimate scale,
devoid of overt symbolism or spiritual connotations but suffused
with a sense of organic interaction, of process, change and growth □

Asher Brown Durand
In the Woods 1855
60¾″ × 48″
The Metropolitan Museum
of Art

1856), who shared Cole's love of nature and traveled extensively throughout the north-east United States in pursuit of the landscape of mood. Doughty was born in Philadelphia and worked in the leather business there until 1820, when he decided to become a landscape painter. He settled in Boston in 1832 after traveling through Pennsylvania, New York and New England, finally moving to New York in 1841. A visit to England in 1837 brought him into contact with the English landscape tradition and this had a strong effect on his work. His painting *A River Glimpse*, made after this journey, shows reminiscences of the work of John Constable in the handling of the foliage and the use of color. It is a landscape of calmness and serenity, unlike the more vibrant vistas of Thomas Cole.

In spite of the American artists' conviction of the beauty of their national landscape, Asher B. Durand (1796–1886) was the only one who worked directly from the subject. He was probably the first American to ignore the common practice of working in the studio from sketches done in the open air. In addition to preliminary sketches he also made detailed painted studies outdoors with the result that his landscapes filled up with detail, becoming realistic rather than idealized. His early training as an engraver is a further reason for the amount of detail included in his painting.

Durand was a close friend of Cole and on the latter's death he painted the picture *Kindred Spirits* as a memorial to him. Not only was the painting documentary in showing Cole with William Cullen Bryant, with whom he often traveled to contemplate the grandeur and mystery of the landscape, but it was also allegorical in drawing a parallel between the views of Cole and Bryant on landscape, philosophy and religion. With the death of Cole Durand became the leading artist of the Hudson River School but prior to his success as a painter he was probably America's most successful engraver, working not only on engravings of such works as Trumbull's *Declaration of Independence* but also on banknote design and production. His fame as an engraver drew him into the group of people involved in establishing the National Academy of Design in New York and he moved among the New York cultural and intellectual elite. His patron in the 1830s was Luman Reed, who together with him was instrumental in persuading Cole to produce *The Oxbow* and who also commissioned from Cole the series *The Course of Empire*. Under the encouragement of Reed much of Durand's work at this time was in portraiture and figure painting, but gradually the number of landscape paintings increased until almost all his work was in this genre.

In 1840 Durand visited London and traveled on through Europe, discovering and admiring the work of Claude Lorraine, Salvator Rosa and the Dutch painters. His work developed from the ideal towards the real and in his painting *In the Woods* (1855) we see Durand's interest in the natural elements of landscape. The progression of his work towards the specific is the result of his working directly from the motif out of doors. In this painting our attention is concentrated on the detail of the foreground objects, on the diagonal trees leaning inward from either side and on the fallen tree forming the base of this triangle. In this respect the painting differs greatly from Cole's idealized romantic vistas. Durand's habit of working out of doors is a significant one in that it is contemporary with, or possibly predates, the similar practice in France of the Barbizon group working outside Paris in the Forest of Fontainebleau. However, Durand did not slavishly follow the motif; his work continued to use the compositional ideas shared by other members of the Hudson River School.

Where Cole's work bears traces of the Italianate classical landscape tradition, and Doughty's style is in the mold of the English Romantic School, Asher B. Durand's work bears comparison with that of the Dutch seventeenth-century masters and with the early European Romantic tradition. His style is fundamentally Baroque in its dramatic mechanisms, false lighting and exaggerated effects while retaining a convincing aura of naturalism and truth to nature.

There is undoubtedly also a symbolic quality in his work, not as clearly stated as that used by Cole, but similar in its overall effect; this creates a sense of the all-powerful creative force in nature, beyond Man's grasp, before which mere mortals can only stand aghast. This superbly contrived and detailed composition blends all these aspects in an overwhelming cocoon-like vision of a wild yet benevolent nature. The immensely subtle draftsmanship and controlled use of light and tonality derived from Durand's training as a steel engraver and illustrator – a background which, it seems, in no way belittled his facility as a colorist □

The tradition of romantic landscape was continued into the third quarter of the nineteenth century by a younger group of painters, of whom Jasper F. Cropsey (1823–1900) was the closest adherent to its characteristics. Trained as an architect, Cropsey practiced for five years before giving up architecture in favor of landscape painting in 1841. As was customary with American artists he went on the Grand Tour to Europe, returning to New York in 1849. His early work is very close to Cole's and he drew from the same sources until his return to England in 1856. Here, in 1860, he produced *Autumn on the Hudson* which is often considered to be his best piece and which earned him considerable fame in England and even led to his being granted an audience with Queen Victoria. In spite of its fame, this painting is not as successful as some of his smaller works. Its emphasis on a linear style of painting and the use of intense color produce

The influence of the Hudson River School – not only the stylistic bravura and epic quality of their work but also the way in which their view of the American landscape was imbued with an heroic mythic quality – was to linger for many years as a central aspect of the American Dream image. Many painters of the next generation pursued these various aspects of the Hudson River School style, and developed them to the verge of caricature. But in order to achieve such effects great technical assurance was a prerequisite.

The work of George Inness contains very fine examples of this combination of technical finesse and bold myth-making. In the absence of any action, Inness could draw upon the long tradition of European classical landscape painting to imbue a straightforward scene such as this with qualities comparable (though less robust) to those of Turner. The trick was in the light effects, gilding the landscape with a golden evening glow which transformed the basic constituents of the scene – the river, cattle, trees and clouds – into a poetic and nostalgic eulogy □

disjointed passages which detract from the overall structure of the work.

English views followed, as well as anecdotal pieces reminiscent of some of Cole's work. He returned to the United States in 1863 and *Greenwood Lake* (1875) belongs to this late stage. In this picture we see many of the characteristics of the Hudson River School, with the picturesque elements of shattered tree trunk, the central stretch of water and the distant hills.

Luminism

The Hudson River School did not stop with Cole, Doughty, Durand and followers such as Cropsey. Many artists started within its parameters and developed along other lines in much the same way that the post-Impressionists in France grew out of Impressionism.

George Inness
Autumn Meadows 1869
30″ × 45½″
The Metropolitan Museum of Art

George Inness (1825–1894) was a great admirer of the early Hudson River School. His *Autumn Meadows* of 1869 owes much to Cole but even more, in its understanding of light, to Claude Lorraine, whose work Inness had seen on his visits to Europe in the 1840s and the 1850s. In its emphasis on light it is close to the work of a group of artists who developed from the Hudson River School and painted in a style which has become known as Luminism.

The label of Luminism refers to those painters who were concerned with depicting the naturalism of light. It was, in a way, a natural progression from the work of Asher B. Durand. Like the Hudson River School, Luminism is not descriptive of a school of painters with the same aims; it is rather a means of identifying a tendency in a range of artists from the gentle images of Kensett to the almost frozen paintings of Lane and the grandiose images of Bierstadt. The common element is a concentration on the effects of light at the expense of the Hudson River School's interest in the picturesque. It is very difficult, if not impossible, to separate these painters from the Hudson River School and probably the division is too arbitrary. It would be more realistic to see Luminism as an aspect of the Hudson River School – a progression from, but not a reaction against, it. Sanford Robinson Gifford (1823–1880), for example, could easily be classified as Hudson River School for his early work is so close to Cole's. His paintings gradually concentrated more on the aerial perspective of distant views of mountains, peaceful water and sunsets, imitating the atmospheric effects by repeated glazes of linseed oil and transparent pigment. The softness of the image that he produced in this way did not meet with universal acclaim, some critics attacking him for submerging his sensitive observations under his 'applied atmosphere'.

Gifford traveled widely in both America and Europe and, after his second European trip, he painted *Kauterskill Clove* in 1862. This is compositionally similar to many Hudson River School paintings, with the tall foreground tree on the left breaking the horizon line and the vast vista stretching out before us. However, there the similarity ends and we see veils of atmosphere interposed between us and the distant view, while the foreground is bathed in glowing orange light. In spite of this change in emphasis, like other Hudson River painters before him he composed the landscape in his studio from outdoor studies.

One of the most financially successful and influential of this second generation of Hudson River School painters was John F. Kensett (1816–1872) who, as a student, traveled with Durand to Europe. On his return to New York in 1847 he soon became acquainted with the art elite and was accepted into city society. In spite of his visit to Europe his work was completely committed to the American landscape and showed scarcely a trace of his experiences abroad.

As a former student of Durand's, Kensett followed his example and took all his equipment on his painting tours throughout the north-east and beyond in order to work in the open air directly from the subject. His early work shows a characteristically Hudson River School style, with the picturesque elements being of primary importance. His colors were always within a limited range and by the time of *Passing Off of the Storm*, painted in the last year of his life, they have become subdued and restricted to three horizontal bands of greys and bluish greys defining the clouds, the dark sky and the water. Within this simple structure the accents of light and dark in the shapes of boats and a small island lead us through the seascape and articulate the surface of the painting. It is interesting to compare this work to the horizontal bands of color of the twentieth-century artist Mark Rothko.

These coastal scenes appear almost compositionless and reject completely any traces of Hudson River School ideas. In them Kensett is reacting to a specific scene at a specific moment, capturing the effects of light and mood. The concept here is very similar to Impressionist painting, yet the result is very different. Where the Impressionists abandoned the restrictions of the outlines of the objects portrayed and executed everything in the same broken patches of color, the Luminists like Kensett never made that philosophical leap and the objects are still defined.

Comparisons between the Luminists and the French Impressionists also spring to mind when we look at the paintings of Martin Johnson Heade (1819–1904), especially his series on haystacks such as *Newbury Port Meadows* (1876–81) and *Sudden Shower, Newbury*

Sanford Robinson Gifford
Kauterskill Clove 1862
48″ × 39⅞″
The Metropolitan Museum of Art

B oth Thomas Doughty and George Inness relied heavily upon the manipulation of light to achieve their effects. But the two artists represent two very different approaches – the former working from the close observation of light, the latter introducing a poetic suffusion of dramatic, almost theatrical, lighting effects. In this, Inness approached a style known as Luminism, in which light effects were used to enhance the landscape with a mystical, mythical and quasi-spiritual aura.

In this painting Sanford Robinson Gifford deploys a similarly dramatic lighting effect, complemented by sensitive handling of local and distant atmospheric effects, to create an immensely powerful and elegiac view across the Catskill Mountains. To achieve this end Gifford also exploited the sheer scale and extent of the panoramic vision available to him, hinting not for the first time at that enduring theme of American art, the distant frontier, the evasive, indistinct prospect of human aspiration and promise which was offered by the New World □

Marsh (1867–75). Heade's travels took him to the tropical regions of Florida and to South America, where he worked in Brazil on a series of illustrations of orchids, passion flowers and hummingbirds for a projected book. Some of his paintings, notably *Thunderstorm over Narragansett Bay* (1868) and *The Coming Storm* (1859), exploit the dramatic aspect of nature, with the dark skies turning the water black. The extreme coloring of these paintings was not favorably received by the critics of the day, although interest in his work was reawakened when it was included in the Museum of Modern Art's exhibition 'Romantic Painting in America' in 1942.

Heade's fascination with changing light effects is probably best seen in the haystacks series of Newbury Port meadows. In these, and in his other marsh scenes, he chose a long horizontal format and although painted on a small scale they express the monumentality of the landscape. Though there is no reason to assume a connection, it is interesting to compare Heade's haystack series, such as *Sudden Shower, Newbury Marsh* (1867–75), with Monet's series of haystacks painted a few years later. Whereas Monet dissolved all the forms in his overall color and broken brushwork Heade retained the definition of the

John Frederick Kensett
Passing Off of the Storm
1872
11⅜" × 24½"
The Metropolitan Museum of Art

*B*y the middle of the nineteenth century, the post-Romantic
achievements of the naturalist and realist painters in Europe –
especially those of Corot, the Barbizon school, Manet, Boudin and
their contemporaries in Italy, Germany and Scandinavia – were
being felt in the United States. Of course, many American artists
traveled and studied in Europe (Kensett among them) but this was
also a period which saw the beginnings of a great wave of European
emigration – especially from Germany and Scandinavia – to the
Americas, the immigrants bringing with them fresh ideas and
outgoing sensibilities.

   Kensett's view of becalmed sailing vessels is an early example of
a theme which proved tremendously popular in the later nineteenth
century North East–maritime painting. It has much of the stillness
and balance to be found in contemporary Italian realism (this is
hardly surprising given the fact that Kensett studied in Rome for
some time) and a knowing balance of color, light and deft graphic
notation of details to be found in the work of Isabey, Boudin and
Corot □

objects. Like Kensett, Heade has divided *Sudden Shower, Newbury Marsh* into definite horizontal tonal bands but has included much more information in the way of detail. The horizontal banding has been interrupted by leading the viewer into the painting by the use of the winding river and by the disposition of the shapes of the haystacks.

Unlike Kensett, the studio sale of whose paintings at his death realized over $130,000, Heade was not financially successful and he seems to have drifted into obscurity in Florida. Only now is the quality and importance of his painting fully recognized.

The classic rectilinear structure of Luminist paintings appears at its most obvious in the work of Fitz Hugh Lane (1804–65). Elements are abstracted and details are hardened to reject the changing character of nature in favor of a 'frozen' reality, as in *Stage Fort across Gloucester Harbor* (1862). If we look at Lane's preliminary drawings for his paintings there is evidence that horizontal and vertical points were plotted very carefully and accurately; it is this linear relationship that gives the pictures a sense of calm and order similar to the characteristics of early Renaissance painting and to the work of Seurat in the late nineteenth century in France.

Mainly self-taught, Lane, like many artists of this period, worked in the printing business as a lithographer in Boston before turning to painting. He then founded his own lithography business, reproducing his many seascapes which were much in demand.

Lane's paintings are based on drawings made out of doors and the restrictions imposed by his lameness probably contributed to the peculiar characteristics of his paintings. In

Martin Johnson Heade
Lynn Meadows 1863
12" × 30½"
Yale University Art Gallery

*T*he marked and dramatic use of heightened colors, even in
otherwise naturalistic treatments of landscape views, would
betray the continuing influence of Romanticism beneath the surface
of mainstream American painting up to the early years of the
twentieth century. The more extreme examples tended to follow the
progress of the Frontier westwards, where the great physical
challenge and natural splendor of the new Continent matched the
style. Nevertheless strong Romantic coloring even informed works
which were in other respects analytic and naturalistic to a degree
comparable with Impressionist practice. Heade's meticulous
attention to detail and to local light and color effects together with
the broad vistas of his compositions provided him with the means to
establish a feeling of monumentality and resonance in quite
unremarkable or impoverished landscape subjects □

**Fitz Hugh Lane
Stage Fort Across
Gloucester Harbour** 1862
38″ × 60″
The Metropolitan Museum
of Art

his drawings he aligned all objects to the horizon and often produced a panoramic sketch as a preparation for more than one painting, working on long sheets of paper pasted together. From this long strip he then selected segments for each painting. Perhaps his graphic printing experience had some impact on the final linear style but his training, or rather lack of it, is probably of greater importance in that there are traces of a conceptual primitivism in his work. Any sense of naivety is tempered by the sophistication of the subtle range of light, but the clear delineation of form is like that found in the primitive self-taught painters. In some of his oil sketches Lane ventured away from the rigidly delineated image towards a much more painterly Impressionistic approach but these excursions are rare and the majority of his work falls within Luminist parameters.

*T*he work of Fitz Hugh Lane marks an interesting intersection
of various strands in Romantic American art. This style was
essentially naive and this characterizes his graphic and
compositional sense. But, like many naives, the intensity of his
realization of imagery, his lack of compositional or pictorial
movement, and his reduction of forms to essentials, created a strange
and forceful atmosphere. This was enhanced by his use of a
similarly naive Luminism which looks back to its roots in the work
of Washington Allston and beyond that to the baroque painter,
Claude Lorraine. The cumulative impact however looks forward to
the work of Hopper and Sheeler in the 1920s.

Any feeling of disquiet or threat in Lane's landscapes is diffused
by his introduction of people as central elements in the landscape.
These figures are everyday and familiar, and for the first time we see
human activity as an intrinsic aspect of the American scene – people
as part of the landscape rather than overpowered by it □

Realism

The growth of national pride in the era of President Jackson encouraged the depiction of the American wilderness and the development of the landscape schools; it also encouraged the recording of the American people, at work and at leisure. The realism of these genre paintings appealed to the American people and opened up a new market for artists. This style was something that attracted a very wide audience, since it required no prior knowledge of art and no understanding of aesthetic sensibilities, and it was fostered by such companies as Currier and Ives of New York who reproduced many of these paintings as lithographs which found a ready market in nineteenth-century America. The scale of this market can be appreciated by the fact that between 1835 and 1907 Currier and Ives lithographed over 4300 subjects which sold for between 20 cents and $3 per copy.

William Sidney Mount (1807–1868) was one of the artists whose paintings were lithographed for the mass market by Currier and Ives, but he was more than a producer of popular prints. As a friend of Cole's he accompanied him on many of his sketching trips and developed a strong interest in landscape painting. He was born and brought up on Long Island, studied for a while in New York in a sign painting shop and then with a portrait painter, but returned to Long Island to paint the landscape that he loved. His study of old masters was not, as for most American artists, learned from a Grand Tour of Europe but from paintings that he saw in New York, especially the work of the Dutch painters. This influence can be seen in the tonal and color range of his painting and especially in his use of light, and it is the latter which allies him to the Luminist school.

Mount's paintings show romanticized rural scenes in which the emphasis is on the nostalgia of country life without any indication of its hardships. (This type of nostalgia can also be found in the English tradition of Morland and Wilkie, whose work also appeared as popular prints.) Anecdotal aspects are an important part of his work – for example, *Bargaining for a Horse* (1835), *Farmers Nooning*, showing farm laborers resting on a haystack, or *The Power of Music* (1847), depicting a country fiddler in a barn with an audience of farm workers while a negro worker stands outside and listens. The understanding of the social problems confronting blacks in America is tackled in several of Mount's paintings, expressing their humanity and yet their separation from the white society which surrounds them.

His rendering of the effects of light is possibly seen at its best in *Long Island Farmhouses* (1862), a study of his neighbor's home. Light suffuses the landscape and the anecdotal aspect of children at play is relegated to a minor part of the painting.

Mount was not the provincial painter he is sometimes considered to be. Like several other artists such as Thomas Eakins, Samuel F. B. Morse and Charles Wilson Peale, he was an inventor of some ability and his interest in science and mathematics is evidenced in his comprehensive library collection. His anecdotal paintings are more than a search for nostalgia – they often address mathematical problems of handling forms in space which are comparable to equivalent concerns in the work of Piero della Francesca in fifteenth-century Italy. The similarity in structure of Piero della Francesca's *Flagellation of Christ* is close to the formal conclusions reached by Mount in *The Power of Music*; yet in spite of his intellectual approach to the formal problems of his work, Mount is best known for his democratic exhortation to artists to paint for the many and not for the few.

An artist who late in life broke with the early ideas of the Hudson River School in favor of the Luminist vision was Thomas Worthington Whittredge (1820–1910). Whittredge traveled widely in Europe, supported by his patron Nicholas Longworth and ten others, settling in Düsseldorf from 1849 to 1856 where he met the artist Emanuel Leutze. In Switzerland he made the acquaintance of Albert Bierstadt and subsequently lived in Rome with him and Sanford Robinson Gifford. His travels also took him to the American West with Kensett and Gifford and the effect of his wanderings is evident in the variety of his early work.

Whittredge's mature style is seen in *The Camp Meeting* (1874), where the light is now the subject, and his handling of it approaches the luminosity of early Impressionism. The actual 'meeting' is relegated to the distant landscape set within the woodland and he uses the glow of light seen through the darkness of the forest and the reflections in the

William Sidney Mount
Long Island Farmhouses
1862–3
21⅞″ × 29⅞″
The Metropolitan Museum of Art

B y the middle years of the nineteenth century the East Coast had
 become (and was suddenly recognized as being) what
Americans for generations had dreamed of owning – an historical
landscape. The emergence of painters – Lane and William Sidney
Mount among them – who celebrated this, not in overtly historical
paintings but rather in comfortable genre views, proved enormously
popular. Mount's work was recognized as a record of a unique
American heritage, and his paintings were lithographed by Currier
and Ives for mass distribution. His choice of subjects identified those
motifs which remain at the heart of the historical American Dream
landscape – most notably the farm and the homestead. These are
recognizably family homes of some vintage, still worked and
lovingly maintained by the descendants of their original owners.

Mount's style is prosaic and populist, not naive like that of
Lane, but rather in the honorable tradition of the journeyman
illustrator which, with the development of popular prints and of
illustrated journals, remained a vital and dearly loved aspect of the
American art scene right up to the works of, say, Norman Rockwell
in our own day. Mount's appealing interpretation of the countryside
evokes the more attractive aspects, masking the real hardship and
deprivations of contemporary country life □

foreground water to give the painting a sense of freshness. This painting is reminiscent of Martin Johnson Heade in its long horizontal format, its feeling of tranquility, and in the sensuousness of the glowing light.

In all the painting of this time there was a strong sentiment for recording untamed nature – a landscape untouched by man – typified by Thomas Cole's omission of the railroad in his *View on the Catskill, Early Autumn* of 1837. Samuel Colman (1832–1920) interrupts the nostalgia of the period and in his painting *Storm King on the Hudson* (1866) shows steam transport barges on the Hudson River, contrasting them with sailboats in the distance and rowing boats in the foreground. All of the boats are held in the picture plane by the strong vertical reflections and the dominant horizontal of the far bank. The emphasis, as in all Luminist paintings, is on light and Colman exploits the storm clouds gathering over the mountains to link them with the smoke from the steam barge. In the integration of smoke and clouds and the unifying effects of light there is evidence of a knowledge of Turner's landscapes.

In this painting Colman managed to create a harmonious work depicting the man-made and the natural throughout the picture and produced a work of pearly tints reminiscent of the light quality of the seventeenth-century French painter, Claude Lorraine. The vertical and horizontal underlying structure is typical of the Luminist painters as seen in the work of Fitz Hugh Lane.

Colman traveled in Europe in 1860–2 and again in 1871–5, this time visiting North Africa as well. As a result of these travels he became interested in more exotic subjects but

Worthington Whittredge
The Camp Meeting 1874
16″ × 40 1/16″
The Metropolitan Museum
of Arts

*O*ne of the natural developments of the Luminist School was
towards pure Impressionism and many American artists who
traveled to Europe – such as Whistler, Worthington Whittredge and
John Singer Sargent – developed distinctive styles undoubtedly
informed by a direct experience of European Impressionism there.
The influence of Manet and proto-Impressionist works can be felt in
the tension between color and form – finding catharsis in the pure,
almost abstract, manipulation of paint – and in the enormously
broad tonal range and compositional daring of the work.

However, Whittredge here has moved beyond the large, form-
dominated qualities of Manet, and applied the style to a landscape
on a scale Manet would never have dared attempt. In fact few
French Impressionists allowed their primary subject matter to move
beyond the foreground or middle ground and in relegating the
'action' of the painting to the distance, Whittredge comfortably
grafted an Impressionist manner onto the distinctive form of the
American panoramic landscape □

Samuel Colman
Storm King on the Hudson
1866
32⅛″ × 59⅞″
National Museum of
American Art, Smithsonian
Institution

this painting *Storm King on the Hudson*, although painted after his first visit abroad, reverts to the landscape that occupied him for the ten years prior to his departure.

God Revealed in Nature

The romantic landscapes of Thomas Cole and the Hudson River School were converted in the paintings of Frederic E. Church (1826–1900) and Albert Bierstadt (1830–1902) into the grandiose synthesis of realism and spirituality. Church was Cole's only pupil, spending two years from 1844–6 with him at Catskill before moving to New York. His reliance on Cole's romantic form of composition was soon abandoned in favor of a greater emphasis on naturalism in the depiction of the local landscape, in a style closer in fact to Asher B. Durand's. His interest in theology led him to focus on dramatic symbols of God's power – impressive natural phenomena in landscape – believing that God reveals himself most clearly in such manifestations. Church's search for the most arresting natural forms

*T*his astonishing painting bears an obvious, and intentional
similarity to Turner's The Fighting Temeraire, *whilst
demonstrating with true American phlegm and pragmatism the
positive qualities of the natural American scene, untainted by the
foreboding notions of industrialism and decay which undermine
Turner's vision. In other respects the concerns are similar: smoke
and atmospheric effects, the peculiar reflective and light-enhancing
qualities of the open water, the juxtaposition of bellowing
machinery and natural beauty are common to both paintings.*

*This comparison however brings to light a fundamental
difference between the English and the American landscape schools;
although often similar in choice of subjects and the intensity of
vision, the English painters tended to demonstrate a single-minded
concentration on the central elements of their art. The Americans,
perched still on the eastern seaboard of a vast continent, placed their*

*vision within a vista of open, limitless and unparalleled
opportunities. And it was in landscape painting that this promise
came most clearly into focus, most nearly into experienced reality* □

led him to travel widely throughout Europe, America and the Middle East. The paintings he produced after an expedition to South America established his reputation.

Church is best known for the very large landscapes, especially his painting of *Niagara* (1857), in which his handling of light is close to the Luminist painters. As we have seen, Niagara had been a popular image of nationalism in the United States since 1800 and the horizontal format of this painting owes its origins to the panoramas of such artists as Trumbull. However, it differs from these early images in thrusting the viewer into the landscape. Trumbull's painting shows the Falls in the center distance, with banks

forming the right and left of the canvas in a classic manner; Church, on the other hand, abandoned these compositional rules in an attempt to show the magnificence of the image and the immense, awe-inspiring force of the waters.

Church precipitates the spectator into the picture by removing foreground emphasis on detail, putting it throughout the picture instead, and by using a novel compositional arrangement. The rendering of light is masterly and the painting of the rainbow rising from the water vapor of the falls gained especial praise from John Ruskin, the most influential art critic of England in the nineteenth century, who likened Church to Turner.

Anon
Blondin Crossing Niagara
Falls on a Tightrope c. 1859
New York Historical Society

The half-century or so which divide this anonymous painting from the wondrous view of the Niagara Falls by John Vanderlyn (page 9) was a period in which the figments and the landscape of the American Dream began to undergo a major transformation. The landscape of New England and the Eastern States was now largely familiar, indeed Colman's Storm King on the Hudson *presents a landscape no longer wild and now redolent of human history. Natural wonders were still there (despite the enormous growth in population – between 1800 and 1860 over 5 million European emigrants had arrived – the American landscape was still largely untouched), but were less an object of awed fascination than essential sights on the itinerary of that great American creature – the tourist. Blondin's famous publicity stunt was symptomatic of the decline in the Romantic appeal of the Eastern landscape. It was to the West, in the vanguard of the Frontier, that new American myths would now be wrought* □

In his late, large-scale works the influence of Turner became more evident and the scale became intensified into a tendency toward melodrama.

The rainbow was often seen as a symbol of the New World, implying hope, a new beginning and a token of God's covenant, and Church used this consciously, not only for its image as a powerful natural phenomenon but also for its inherent symbolism. *Niagara* established Church as a major figure in the art world and in the minds of the general public. His work was publicized in newspapers and his one-man exhibitions were overwhelmed with visitors – thus increasing the price of his paintings. In such large canvases as *Niagara* and *Heart of the Andes* (1859) Church filled the surface of the painting with minute detail, but this in no way detracts from the overall structure of the painting. These epic images were carefully composed works executed in the studio but based on a

*T*he passages to the Midwest and West from the Eastern seaboard were twofold: the difficult overland routes across the Allegheny and Appalachian Mountains, or the more leisurely, salubrious and secure passage by steamer from the headwaters of the Mississippi basin south and east to the Great Divide itself – the beginning of the Midwest. Before the advent of the railroads, the riverboat and the covered wagon were the twin workhorses of the great Westward migration.

The rich coalfields of Pennsylvania were the powerhouse of early nineteenth-century American industry, but both the riverboat, with its shallow draft and huge paddlewheels, and the large American steam locomotive were designed to burn timber in their furnaces. This meant that neither was reliant upon a complex of supply or service depots, and they became the ideal tools for forcing a passage across difficult, uninhabited territory. By 1870 the rapid growth of the railroad network had largely supplanted the elegant riverboats, although many remained in use further west, on the upper waters of the Missouri, the Arkansas and the Red rivers □

great many preliminary drawings and oil sketches made in situ.

In the later years of his life the technical expertise of these large-scale works diminished in popularity and he concentrated on oil sketches on paper and canvas. These display a remarkable fluidity and spontaneity which he had sometimes lost when scaling them up to his large canvases.

While Church created impressive canvases of East Coast and foreign landscapes his contemporary Albert Bierstadt explored an area neglected by artists so far – the American West – on a similarly epic scale. Bierstadt was born in Germany and moved to Massachusetts as a child in 1832, but his interest in painting took him back to Düsseldorf in 1853. Later studies led him to Rome with Worthington Whittredge in 1856 before he returned to the United States.

J. V. Cornell
Steam Boat "Iron Witch"
c.1846
New York Historical Society

The mid-nineteenth century was a time of exploration of the West and the expeditions took artists with them to make maps and record in sketches the country that they passed through. Bierstadt joined an expedition led by Colonel Frederick W. Lander, whose aim was to map a route to California via the Rocky Mountains. The sketches that Bierstadt brought back to the East Coast served as the foundation for his vast canvases of the Western landscapes. With these his reputation was established and he made a further Western tour in 1863. Bierstadt was probably the most successful artist of this period financially – his large canvases fetched up to $35,000 each – and he was able to build himself a large mansion on the Hudson where he enjoyed a lavish lifestyle.

His paintings show an interest in light comparable to that of the Luminists; however, in their epic scale they are closer to the paintings of Frederic E. Church. In *Among the Sierra Nevada Mountains, California* (1868), the grandeur of the mountains is accented by the glittering light on the waterfall as it cascades into the lake. The inclusion of the small herd of deer by the foreground edge of the lake affirms the sense of calm and enhances the poetry of the image. No human figures impinge upon the solitude of the virgin land. The lighting is not so dramatic in *Rocky Mountains, Lander's Peak* (1863), but the scale is similar;

The difficulties confronting early immigrants as they set out from the Arkansas Post or Kansas City on the long trek across the Great Plains were simply horrific: starvation, exposure, hostile Indians and disease were common currency; murder, robbery and cannibalism daily events. A major problem was disorientation arising from the unrelieved flatness of the Midwest landscape. For those fortunate enough to reach the Rocky Mountains, their problems were just beginning. Of course, many settled the plains, but the overland route to California and the Pacific Coast held the constant fascination of a new Promised Land. The Mormons under Brigham Young found theirs in the unlikeliest of settings, at Salt Lake City.

The paintings produced by Alfred Bierstadt from sketches made while accompanying a surveying expedition did much to foster the Promised Land myth. The glorification of the landscape on this scale, although impressive and beautiful in pictorial terms, did little to convey the very real hardships encountered by the majority of Europeans who passed this way □

the whole landscape is awe-inspiring and far removed from the early Hudson River School. In this picture Bierstadt has included an Indian encampment showing the scale of the mountainous landscape and reflecting the romantic feelings of the time towards the push West.

By 1830 the Indians had been either exterminated or driven beyond the Mississippi. In their remoteness from the eastern seaboard they were no longer thought of as a threat or a hindrance to progress but rather the reverse. They were seen as part of the natural landscape – the noble savage – and their inclusion in Bierstadt's *Rocky Mountains, Lander's Peak* asserts this sentiment. In 1808 John Trumbull had included the Indian group in his painting of Niagara Falls for similar picturesque and romantic reasons.

Probably the first great painter of Indians was George Catlin (1796–1872), who over the period of six years made several journeys to the West and chronicled many of the Indian tribes. His best-known works are the numerous portraits of Indians, although he was not interested in them as individuals. He had an unlimited curiosity about everything that he saw in his travels, including the landscapes, Indians, buffalos and the interaction of all these elements. *Buffalo Chase in Winter, Indians on Snowshoes* (1830–9) shows this

**Albert Bierstadt
The Rocky Mountains,
Lander's Peak** 1863
73½″ × 120¾″
The Metropolitan Museum
of Art

*T*he American myth has always been closely related to wealth, and Americans have always been willing to pay handsomely to have their dreams brought to life. Alfred Bierstadt's style, which perfectly complemented his majestic subjects, was a carefully balanced cocktail of theatrical and pictorial effect, the success of which made him one of the wealthiest painters of his day. The enormous scale of his paintings matched the scope of his vision. He conveyed the sheer size of his mountainous scenery by organizing the landscape into fairly flat recessive planes, alternately darkened or highlighted in a manner similar to stage lighting. The viewer's eye is drawn from picturesque foreground details, painted in a style of heightened realism, through successive contrasting passages of color,

light and movement to a distant and misty evocative backdrop where peaks soar into the cloudy ether, the landscape all but dissolving into the sky.

Bierstadt's eye for detail and taste for the dramatic is almost too much to take in, creating a sense of other-worldliness which bears comparison with his countryman and forebear, Casper David Friedrich. Bierstadt remains undoubtedly the finest of the second generation of American Romantic landscapists, a worthy successor to the Hudson River School, and a myth-maker of the first order □

Albert Bierstadt
Among the Sierra Nevada
Mountains, California 1868
72″ × 120″
National Museum of
American Art, Smithsonian
Institution

*B*y the time Bierstadt produced his views of the Rocky Mountains, the native Indians were already being confined to reservations, many of them in this harsh upland environment far from their original homes on the plains and riverbasins of the Midwest. In 1869, when the railroad reached the Rockies, the Great Plains – historic home of the buffalo, the Indian's economic base – were irrevocably split in two, and the herds began to dwindle rapidly. This was the beginning of the real end for the American Indian. George Catlin was fortunate enough to see and record something of the way of life of the Plains Indians before this tragic episode got under way. He painted them without affectation, with an almost anthropological interest in their customs, habits and day-

to-day life. And yet his work retains a strongly decorative and whimsical quality which sets it apart from pure journalism and gives a unique magical quality to his views of the Midwest □

interaction. It is freely painted and the fluidity of handling underlines the movement of the figures and animals. The hunt takes place in a simple, stark, snow-covered land with a sky enlivened by the inclusion of billowing clouds in the top right.

Catlin was not only a painter/historian but also an entrepreneur, and in the culture of the American Indian he saw a source of great potential income. He took Indian artifacts and even Indians back to the East and abroad to Europe, exhibiting them along with his paintings in a forerunner of the Wild West show that Buffalo Bill Cody was to take on tour later in the century. The Indian race was commonly seen as a doomed culture and Catlin never fully reconciled his interest in helping them to survive with his desire to make money by exploiting them. His attempts to persuade the US government to purchase his Indian Gallery intact were unsuccessful and his paintings and Indian artifacts were finally exchanged to pay off his enormous debts in 1852. However, his journey to Europe had had an important impact on some French painters who saw in the American Indian Rousseau's concept of the noble savage and the Romantic artist Eugène Delacroix painted these Indians with the same enthusiasm that he had painted the Arabs of North Africa.

A contemporary of Catlin who also made his reputation with his gallery of Indian paintings was John Mix Stanley (1814–1872). Between 1838 and 1850 Stanley traveled as widely as Catlin in his search for subjects, even going as far as Hawaii. In the mid-1830s he had studied with James Bowman, a portrait painter who had trained in Italy, and for two years he produced portraits in and around Chicago. His interest in Indians led him to the West, where he lived for several years in Indian territory, and in 1846 he became the artist for the Colonel Stephen W. Kearny military expedition to California. Like Catlin, Stanley tried but failed to persuade Congress to purchase his large collection of paintings of Indians and their culture. Two large fires, one at the Smithsonian Institute in Washington DC in 1865 and the other at P.T. Barnum's American Museum in New York, destroyed most of his work.

In the paintings that remain we can see how the little academic training that he received from Bowman is used. His studies of landscape are sensitive and capture the effects of light, atmosphere and space but his figures seem to be the result of using pattern books or of working from classical models. This is partly the result of his method of working, for he recorded information on his travels in sketches and by photographs, assembling them to form his compositions in the studio on his return to the East. His painting *Buffalo Hunt on the Southwestern Prairies* (1845) shows the sweeping western landscape but all the buffalos and horses gallop to a set pattern, their legs outstretched rather like those of rocking horses. Similarly his Indians, although reasonably well painted, do not sit convincingly on their horses. Yet in spite of these drawbacks he was very conscious of composition, placing figures and objects to lead the eye through the painting. Stanley probably knew the Indians and the Western territories better than the other artists working in this genre since he spent so much of his mature life exploring and recording, and traveled as resident artist on government expeditions in the 1840s and 1850s. The practice of having an artist accompany expeditions was customary at this time and painters such as Worthington Whittredge, Sanford Robinson Gifford and John Kensett joined various military explorations through Colorado and the Rocky Mountains to New Mexico.

When the German naturalist Prince Alexander Philip Maximilian von Wied-Neuwied visited the United States to chart the West and document the Indian tribes he encountered, he brought with him as his resident artist Karl Bodmer (1809–1893). Bodmer was a young Swiss artist in his early twenties who had trained in Zurich and Paris.

The paintings that he produced during this period were meant for reproduction as illustrations but they are also important as works of art in their own right. His *Mih-Tutta-Hang-Kusch, Mandan Village*, which shows Indians approaching Fort McKenzie in the dead of winter, is full of vitality in its drawing of the foreground group of Indians and the scrub undergrowth and it captures the sense of the sweeping plain with the straggling line of Indians wandering towards the distant fort. His documentation of the West was done in drawings and in watercolors which were reproduced as colored aquatint illustrations in

George Catlin
Buffalo Chase in Winter,
Indians on Snowshoes
1830–39
24″ × 29″
National Museum of
American Art, Smithsonian
Institution

Maximilian's journal, published in London in 1839–43. This bound collection of polychrome plates is one of the best pictorial historical records of the West. Whereas Catlin was interested in documenting individual Indian figures and Stanley painted studio compositions from notes made during his travels, Bodmer produced studies in watercolor illustrating specific incidents during Maximilian's expedition and this gives them a freshness and vitality that the other paintings lack.

The breadth of the Western landscape which Bierstadt captured so well in his large canvases was the dominant theme of the paintings of Thomas Moran (1837–1926), an Englishman who emigrated to the United States with his parents in 1844, subsequently becoming apprenticed to an engraver in Philadelphia. A return visit to England in 1862 introduced him to the work of J. M. W. Turner, which had a strong and lasting effect on him. He accompanied two government expeditions to Yellowstone and to Colorado in 1870 and 1876 and his resulting chromolithograph illustrations established him as a Western landscapist.

*F*or many on the Frontier, artists and settlers alike, the threat posed to the traditional way of life of the native Indians by mass white settlement was very clear, and was a matter for concern and distress. Not only were irascible Indians a very real source of immediate danger, but more importantly the virtual extermination of largely honorable nations of 'noble savages' was recognized as unethical. The influence such people could bring to bear on the industrialists and politicians of the East was sadly outweighed by the pressure of immigration and of the possibilities open to the white man for exploiting his new continental Eden.

Catlin and John Mix Stanley both exhibited their paintings of the Indian way of life in the cities of the East in an attempt to drum up interest, but their efforts were constantly undermined by largely sensationalist press reports of Indian atrocities and other misinformed propaganda. This tragi-comedy of errors of course reached a climax at Little Big Horn, which finally sealed the fate of the Indians in the American public eye □

From his small sketches Moran produced large, dramatic paintings of the Grand Canyon of the Yellowstone, two of which – *The Grand Canyon of the Yellowstone* (1872) and *The Chasm of the Colorado* (1873) – were bought by Congress for $10,000 each. These paintings were to have a significant impact on the foundation of the national park system in the West.

His small-scale works such as *Cliffs of the Upper Colorado River, Wyoming Territory* (1882) capture the vastness of the Western landscape equally well. This painting, with its strong color and dramatic storm cloud-filled sky, has an energy about it reminiscent of Turner, while Moran's use of the foreground group of Indians as a compositional device to lead the viewer into the picture recalls the romanticism that was evident in the work of Albert Bierstadt. Although painted in his studio, like all his work in oil after his return from the West, its dappled lighting effects and swirling sky give this painting a directness and vitality which suggest it was executed directly from the landscape. This is a very fine painting and Thomas Moran gained deserved recognition during his lifetime; several of

John Mix Stanley
Buffalo Hunt on the South-Western Prairies 1845
60¾″ × 40½″
National Museum of American Art, Smithsonian Institution

his sketching areas were incorporated into the emerging national parks system and his paintings commanded large sums.

Classical Structure Imposed on New World Subjects

Not all paintings of the American West documented the vanishing Indian tribes, nor was all Western art produced by Eastern artists on expeditions. George Caleb Bingham (1811–1879) was born in Virginia and spent his early life in Missouri. His early work shows the limitations of his provincial education but in 1838 he spent three months in Philadelphia studying paintings at the Pennsylvania Academy, after which he visited New York. On his return to Missouri his first version of the *Jolly Flatboatmen* (1846) gained recognition for him by being selected as a frontispiece by the American Art Journal and

10,000 copies of it were engraved. His paintings are about life on the river and also in politics, with which he was closely involved. His active participation in the latter included spending four years painting portraits in Washington DC, but when his party suffered defeat he decided to return to Missouri.

His river scenes are of calm, relaxed moments similar to those images of eastern rural life painted by William S. Mount. Like Mount's, the structure of Bingham's work is strongly classical and he often incorporates the triangular composition favored by many Renaissance artists. In his atmospheric painting *Fur Traders Descending the Missouri* (1845) Bingham positions the boat centrally and parallel to the picture plane. This, together with its rectilinear structure and its emphasis on light, places the painting within the Luminist style and gives it a sense of stability and calmness. The ripples in the water echo

**Karl Bodmer
Mih-Tutta-Hang-Kusch,
Mandan Village** 1833–4
11¼″ × 16⅝″
Joslyn Art Museum, Center for Western Studies, Omaha, Nebraska

*A*t the very point of their demise, the Indians entered the American Dream landscape as an essential aspect of the myth. They had been, of course, an elemental force within the landscape, part of it rather than moving on, across or before it; this was recognized by Catlin and Stanley in a very real sense, and was heroically exploited by Bierstadt.

Here Bodmer's admirable compassion and superficial realism portends something darker. The doleful, dispirited column of straggling Indians is shown approaching Fort Mackenzie on the edge of what was then Nebraska territory and is now Wyoming; the Fort was one of a number guarding the eastern approaches to a crucial settlers trail into the Northern Rockies, and which was at the heart of the Indian wars of the 1870s.

Here the natives are presented as pathetic, and dependent, by implication, upon the white man's beneficence to escape or combat the rigors of a harsh winter climate. What is not acknowledged is that, when left in their own traditional homelands, the Indians had developed perfectly adequate ways of dealing with the extremes of the American environment. But displaced and dispossessed, as here, they became hopeless, fugitive figures, out of touch with a landscape which was becoming increasingly controlled by men from another world □

*T*he vastness of the landscape is comparable to those chosen by
Bierstadt, yet Moran has achieved this sensation on a very
small scale. The painting has a tremendous richness of color and
handling with a vitality reminiscent of the work of Turner whose
work he had studied in England. The foreground group of Indians
leads us into this landscape and provides a picturesque element
while also giving a sense of scale to the scene. The distant tepees,

lightly sketched with pale pigment, emphasize the enormous scale of
the bluffs. There is a marvelous enjoyment of the drama of the
landscape here, with the dappled effects of light in the foreground
and on the bluffs acting as a foil for the swirling cloud-filled sky.
Although based on his expeditions to the West, Bierstadt's
paintings were produced in his studio and show his pictorial
inventiveness – they were not mere topographical copies □

Thomas Moran
Cliffs of the Upper
Colorado River, Wyoming
Territory 1882
16″ × 24″
National Museum of
American Art, Smithsonian
Institution

the horizontal of the boat through the bottom section of the picture. There is an interesting asymmetrical balance in this work; the black cat in the prow of the boat, silhouetted against the strong light on the water, counters the large mass of the figures at the other end of the boat, seen against the darker background area of the distant trees. The figures in the boat are enhanced not only by the strong, clear light which creates solid, three-dimensional forms but also by the use of bold reds and blues for the shirts and trousers; the remainder of the painting is more subdued in color, with softer transitions between shapes.

The painterly stylism of high-brow American nineteenth-century painting, as epitomized by the Hudson School and the Luminist school (originally limited to the East Coast), would soon begin to color and inform the views of paintings produced of more remote regions. In this, the work of Alfred Bierstadt was exceptional but predictable.

In the work of George Caleb Bingham we can see high art notions creeping into areas which were hitherto the province of more instinctive painters such as Catlin, and once again the myth-making process engaged gear. On one level Bingham's work can be regarded, like Catlin's, as a rather esoteric but fairly trustworthy record of sights, scenes and peoples of the Frontier. But in Bingham's paintings we are aware of an additional dimension – most often conveyed by a curious aura of stillness and a delightful Luminist handling of light – which freezes the moment of the scene and transforms it from reportage into an historical idea, resonant with atmosphere and allusive associations which operate outside and beyond the scope of the picture itself □

Bingham's Luminist style did not continue throughout his career. From about 1850 on this clarity of light and form gave way to a more painterly handling – as in *Woodboatmen on a River* (1854) – accompanied by a departure from the classical compositions which draw their influence from the French painter Nicolas Poussin (1594–1665).

With Bingham we see a move away from the enormous vistas of many Western painters to the intimacy of a small group in a Western setting. Through distribution of engravings of his work by the American Art Union Bingham's paintings of river life and Western politics reached a very wide audience.

George Caleb Bingham
Fur Traders Descending
the Missouri 1845
29¼″ × 36¼″
The Metropolitan Museum
of Art

A NEW
REALISM

Winslow Homer
The Veteran in a New Field
1865
24⅛″ × 38⅛″
The Metropolitan Museum
of Art

The Civil War transformed the United States dramatically and virtually instantaneously. Values cherished before the war were discarded in favor of new attitudes resulting from the change to a rapidly expanding industrial culture. The factories that had been developed to service the war continued to strip natural resources from what had previously been wilderness and farmland, and to feed these factories exploitation on a grand scale was launched with profit as the only motive. Centralized areas of production followed as a natural development from the growth of communications and the new industrial steam power processes. The spread of the railroads both absorbed the product of the iron mills and enabled them to flourish by condensing the vast distances between raw resources and industrial centers; within 20 years after the Civil War America had become the major steel manufacturing country in the world. Farming was also affected by this growth of machinery and in the 1860s over 8,000,000 acres of new land came under cultivation in Illinois alone. Cattle ranching expanded over an enormous area, with exports of meat products increasing by over 300 per cent between 1865 and 1880.

Petroleum became a major contributing factor to the economic growth of the nation and by 1870 5,000,000 barrels a year were being produced from the new oil fields. It was an age when the youthful aims of the Republic were submerged beneath unrestrained speculation and mushrooming prosperity which went hand in hand with large-scale public and private corruption.

Along with this new-found wealth went renewed patronage of the arts. European art and decorative styles became the status symbols of these *nouveaux riches* in an attempt to project a respectable image to the outside world. European paintings to match the European style of decor were collected in preference to the work of native artists.

The landscape art recording the westward expansion persisted throughout this period, perpetuating the mythology of the Wild West which was popularized in cheap novels, in exhibitions such as Catlin's Indian Gallery and in Buffalo Bill Cody's Wild West Show. However, much of this expansion was now captured on film as the photographer gradually usurped the role of the painter.

Before the Civil War the art of the United States was a reflection of the life of Americans and their environment and was not overly concerned with theories promulgated by academies. In the post-war era, however, America turned to Europe to acquire 'culture'. The newly-founded Metropolitan Museum of Art in New York and the

*I*t is no accident that the strongest traditions in nineteenth-century Realist art emerged in France and America – both countries which had undergone violent and cathartic revolutions in the closing quarter of the previous century. By Realism we mean art which sees a life-enhancing force in the unidealized everyday condition of mankind – urban or rural, however squalid, mundane or harsh; the fact that the essential stoical nobility of labor was a central motif of Realist art can also be clearly related to the increasing quantity of publications dealing with social politics, culminating in Marx and Engel's Communist Manifesto in 1848.

For Americans, the Civil War of 1861–65 resembled a second Revolution, finally breaking the shackles of the colonial heritage, the new nation emerging like a phoenix from the ashes of the scorched South. The leading force in American Realist art was Winslow Homer, whose early work bears an immediate resemblance to the paintings of the French Realists of the previous generation, notably Courbet and Millet.

One of the great achievements of Realist painting was the discovery of a means of re-examining the fundamental methods of painting. This was in part related to the Realist painters' conscientious rejection of tradition in all its forms, and in part an attempt to create artistic but truthful images in a workmanlike and honest manner □

Museum of Fine Arts in Boston collected art works from all corners of the globe while art students went abroad not just to widen their art experience but to absorb completely the styles of European art. Some of these artists stayed abroad and became justifiably famous as expatriate American artists – James Abbot MacNeill Whistler, John Singer Sargent and Mary Cassatt are the most famous of these. Others returned to the United States and made a significant contribution to the development of American painting with ideas and approaches they brought from Europe, which became modified by native American attitudes.

Not all artists were following European ideas. The Hudson River tradition continued in the work of George Inness, though it was tempered by the ideas of the French Barbizon School. His quiet landscapes were not as noticeable as the grand images of Bierstadt and Church and it was a long time before the American audience recognized the value of his work.

In this post-Civil War period two artists stand out as the foremost American painters in the realist tradition – Winslow Homer and Thomas Eakins. Both men were fiercely independent and uncompromising but, while Homer spent his time in pursuit of the images of rural America, Eakins' life was bound up with the city.

Proto-Impressionism

Winslow Homer (1836–1910) devoted his life to painting and in the latter half of it he moved to Prout's Neck, on the Maine coast, where he lived a solitary existence in a cottage, painting the seascapes that he loved. In his earlier life he had been an artist correspondent for *Harper's Weekly* throughout the Civil War and for several years afterwards. He traveled to Europe in 1867 and in the 1880s but any influence that he absorbed was tempered by his conviction in painting the American scene. He was mainly self-taught, having spent his youth in Boston and Cambridge where at that time there was no art education and no museums. Much of his work for *Harper's Weekly* during the Civil War has a proto-Impressionist quality and we can see this style also in his painting *The Veteran in a New Field*, executed after the end of the war in 1865. There is a painterly quality in the rendering of the wheat field and monumentality in the depiction of the solitary figure of the soldier. This is a strongly designed work, its uncompromisingly central figure breaking through the horizontal divisions of sky, wheatfield and ground. References to the Civil War are seen in the discarded tunic among the fallen wheat. Though there is in Homer's work a strong proto-Impressionist sense in the painterly quality and in the handling of light, he never abandons the solidity of the subject. The figure of the veteran is palpable, with its strong light and shade creating a monumental form.

Winslow Homer
A Game of Croquet 1866
19″ × 30″
Yale University Art Gallery

Winslow Homer
Northeaster 1895
34⅜″ × 50¼″
The Metropolitan Museum of Art

The figure in a landscape acquired, under the brushes of the Realists, a new meaning as an artistic motif. Where the Romantics tended to present humanity as either part of the fabric of the landscape (especially when dealing with the American Indians) or as a minute detail in the overall splendor of nature, the Realists established a dialogue between the human figure and its surroundings. Homer's immense versatility as both a painter and a conceptualist meant that he was able to extend this absorbing dialogue in many different directions.

His favorite motifs included small sailing craft, their crew pitted in an unequal but sporting struggle with the elements. He could adeptly present the working man at one with and yet apart from a landscape of his own making, or present a deceptively tranquil and anodyne image of a genteel garden game. The force of this image however resides in the tension between the genuinely decorative surface of the painting and the visually disturbing contrasts of light and color, the girls' dresses remaining uneasy passages of artificial

brilliance in the all-embracing greenery of their setting. This painting shares a number of similarities with Croquet Scene, *which Homer painted in the same year* ☐

In the late 1860s Homer moved away from the subject of the Civil War to the recreational activities of the middle class and the play of children, many of which works were in the form of wood engravings for *Harper's Weekly*. *A Game of Croquet* (1866) is reminiscent of Monet's painting *Ladies in the Garden* (1866), but while they both share the concept of figures at play in the open air there is a difference in the handling of the solidity of the forms. This early work of Monet's shows his preoccupation with the transient nature of light irrespective of the surface on which it falls; the light on the path and on the grass is the same as that on the figures. Homer, in his recording of the light, never loses sight of the three-dimensionality of the figures as upright forms on a horizontal plane. This version of *A Game of Croquet* is similar to the painting *Croquet Scene*, which Homer also painted in 1866, the year of Monet's *Ladies in a Garden*. In *A Game of Croquet* Homer has removed two figures, a crouching man between the two women and a further man behind the woman on the right, but the pose and costumes of the two remaining women are identical to those in *Croquet Scene*. However, the painting has gained something by the inclusion of a much more interesting background. The solid bank of foliage of *Croquet Scene* has been replaced by a more complex landscape of trees, through which can be seen a distant view, and a greater variety of shape is formed by their positioning and their shadows.

The relation of Homer to Impressionism is interesting in that he seems to have developed his own brand of this before his visit to Paris, based on observation and on his interest in Japanese art which evolved during the years that he produced wood engravings for *Harper's Weekly*. We know very little of Homer's time in Paris and it cannot be established how much he was influenced by the Impressionists. What can be said is that the equilibrium between the perceptual and conceptual approaches to art is one that occupied this American Realist artist from the late 1860s onwards. The *plein air* practice of the French Impressionists was tempered in the United States by the integrity of fact.

Homer's use of space to convey emotional content is evident in his beach scenes such as *High Tide, the Bathers* (1860) and in *Veteran in a New Field*. In *A Game of Croquet* the two figures, though physically related, seem detached from each other emotionally and psychologically. It is a classical composition with carefully plotted positions on horizontals and verticals and this preoccupation with classical design is characteristic of most of his work from the late 1860s onward.

After visits to Tynemouth, England, in 1881 and 1882 (where began his obsession with the sea which would continue after his return to the United States) Homer settled in seclusion in Prout's Neck. In his sea paintings the figure rarely appears and Homer's concern seems to be to reconcile the ephemeral nature of observed atmosphere with his intellectual interest in classical composition. His late work in watercolor shows some influence of Japanese prints, both in the importance he gives to space and also in the sureness of stroke.

American Art

Homer's greatest contemporary was Thomas Eakins (1844–1916), a painter of equal stature though recognition of this came late in life. His approach to his work was scientific, like that of many of the Italian Renaissance painters who developed the concept of the universal man versed in many disciplines rather than restricted solely to painting. Just as these men aimed to record the real world through the pursuit of knowledge so Eakins constructed his paintings on a complex geometrical perspective grid, while in his quest to understand anatomy he dissected corpses at Jefferson Medical College in Philadelphia. Photography also became a tool for Eakins in his attempts to capture reality, assisting him in his analysis of various aspects of it.

We can see the results of his interest in geometrical perspective in his painting *Max Schmitt in a Single Scull*, also known as *The Champion Single Sculls* (1871), where even the ripples in the water are resolved according to a mathematical formula. This is more evident in the preliminary studies for this painting. The subject of sculls was one of Eakins' favorites, allowing him the opportunity of solving the problems of reflected and refracted light in the rippling waters.

Eakins went to Paris in 1866, but he seems not to have been interested in contemporary

Thomas Eakins
Max Schmitt in a Single Scull (The Champion Single Sculls) 1871
32¼″ × 46½″
The Metropolitan Museum of Art

*T*homas Eakins' Realism was not as overt as that of Winslow Homer, nor is it as apparently touched by knowledge of Japanese prints and contemporary French painting. In this it is a step closer to the American scene; the pragmatism of Eakins' art can be related to the same impulse which produced the great American financial, industrial and political dynasties in the last quarter of the nineteenth century. It is indeed art at its most refined and arcane, and as such deals less with the landscape than with those characters – usually specifically named – whose abilities were expended in mastering their environments.

That is not to belittle Eakins' achievement – he is rather the Henry James of American painting to Homer's Melville. Like James, Eakins was quite capable of wonderfully descriptive background passages; here the viewer's attention is demanded and transfixed by Max Schmitt himself, but when the eye wanders the intense, hard-edged naturalism of the central section of the painting gives way to a much looser, more evocative treatment of the surrounding landscape, entranced by his daring handling of the broad expanse of water which fills almost half the canvas □

*O*nce again we see Eakins' protagonists dominating their
environment; however the tension between the principal figure
subjects and their immediate setting has become much more explicit.
The two figures in the boat are both in powerful poses, the dynamics
of their individual actions playing off against one another, forming
a simple but forceful focus to the composition. They are both
painted in considerable detail, the better to hold our attention. But,
before and behind them, Eakins' handling of the foliage, unrelieved
by any distant vista, is astonishingly loose and misty, the colors and
forms of the bullrushes dissolving into a poetic mirage of pure,
almost abstract painting, comparable with Monet's later works in
his water garden at Giverny □

**Thomas Eakins
Will Schuster and
Blackman Going Shooting
(Rail Shooting)** 1876
22⅛″ × 30¼″
Yale University Art Gallery

French artists. He spent three years at the Ecole des Beaux Arts and seems to have absorbed completely the academic training. His paintings combine what is seen by the eye with his knowledge of the natural world and often this form of construction contains elements which detract from the production of a unified painting. *Max Schmitt in a Single Scull*, for example, has some passages of straightforward naturalistic painting in the trees on the left side but Eakins' search for photographic realism in the foreground figure of Max Schmitt produces a portrait so sharply delineated that it isolates it from its surroundings. For both Eakins and Homer this combination of *plein-airisme* and conceptual attitudes produced an art that was specifically American. In Europe at this time the move was towards a greater sense of naturalism, resulting in a more painterly attitude.

The strength of Eakins' work is in his classically-influenced studies of forms in space. The achievement of this through mathematical and photographic resources produces a kind of arrested moment. His studies and paintings of rowing sculls present to us not an impression of movement across water but a frozen motion with echoes of Luminist pictures. Eakins' figures are solidly formed and the strength of the structure of these figures is best seen in studio portraits such as *Amelia C. Van Buren* (1891).

Like many of the artists of this period both in America and Europe Eakins was interested in information gained from photography and he was especially concerned with Muybridge's studies of motion at the University of Pennsylvania in 1884. However, in Europe the camera freed the artist from his prior concern with reality and led him into other areas of visual exploration, resulting in an increased sense of naturalism which engendered interest in the transient nature of light and formed the basis of Impressionism. In America the results were different; the camera became another instrument to reinforce the artist's awareness of his environment. Many American artists of the nineteenth century used photography as a preliminary to painting, including Mount, Lane, Church, Homer and Bierstadt as well as Eakins.

Like several Renaissance artists Eakins was drawn to anatomy and dissected cadavers to extend his knowledge of this subject, which he then incorporated into his paintings. Two paintings draw directly from this experience – *The Gross Clinic* (1875) and *The Agnew Clinic* (1889). These paintings recall Rembrandt's *Anatomy Lesson of Dr Tulp* and, like Rembrandt, Eakins uses the dissection scene as a setting for group portraits.

Eakins' uncompromising attitude to his work extended to his teaching and he insisted on using nude models in his anatomy classes rather than plastercasts of Greek and Roman sculpture as was the practice of the day. These radical methods precipitated his resignation as head of the Pennsylvania Academy when his use of a nude male model in a class of young men and women met with the disapproval of the board of directors.

As in Homer's *A Game of Croquet*, the figure compositions of Eakins have the quality of posed figures transferred into a landscape environment. *Rail Shooting* shows two figures, a white rifleman and a black oarsman, in a marsh setting. The landscape background has a naturalistic atmosphere achieved by working directly from the subject. The figures are 'carved' as forcefully as any marble statue by a strong tonal structure evident most in the white shirt of the black oarsman. This solidity of form, seen in both Homer's and Eakins' work, is a forerunner of the structural configurations used by Cézanne later in the nineteenth century.

There persisted in American art at this time a strong anecdotal element in painting – a kind of homespun philosophy – seen in the work of such artists as Mount and Bingham and popularized by the ubiquitous prints of Currier and Ives. Eastman Johnson (1824–1906) established his reputation in this style with a painting produced around the outbreak of the Civil War which showed a scene of negro life in the South. This painting is now known as *Old Kentucky Home*; the subdued colors and tight control are the result of his training at the Düsseldorf Academy – while in Europe, Johnson also studied the work of Dutch and Flemish painters in The Hague, as well as spending some time in Paris. The next few years brought from Johnson a group of paintings of the struggles of war, but it was after the Civil War that he produced what is now regarded as his best work – a series of landscapes of rural life of which *Cranberry Pickers* (c. 1870–80) is a fine example. The solutions to painting out of doors that he uncovered in some of these pictures is close to

those arrived at by the French Impressionists. Although the figures in these works are as solidly realized as Homer's or Eakins' they do not rely so much on detailed realism but are constructed with patches of light and color in a method which unifies them with the rest of the painting. Unlike the majority of anecdotal painting at this time (including *Old Kentucky Home*) the many studies in this series of *Cranberry Pickers* are devoid of sentiment and are straightforward, honest representations. They have a looseness of brushstroke which is very close to Impressionism but, unlike the Impressionists, Johnson did not consider them as finished paintings. This series is close also to the naturalism of Homer, but has a more sensuous use of pigment.

Johnson's later work is primarily devoted to portraiture and in this way his career came full circle, since he was a painter of politicians before his departure to Düsseldorf. The late paintings such as the *Funding Bill* (1881) are as penetrating as the best of Eakins' work, with echoes of Rembrandt in the warm color and handling of light.

Eastman Johnson
Cranberry Pickers
c. 1870–80
27″ × 54⅛″
Yale University Art Gallery

*T*he turbulent struggle for the continued union of the States of America which, between 1861 and 1865, claimed over 600,000 lives (a higher proportion of losses than any suffered by the armies in the First World War), and the southward and westward surge for agricultural settlement which came in the wake of the war brought about a new and valuable perception of the relationship between man and the land in America. We have already glimpsed this in the work of Winslow Homer. Eastman Johnson's instinctive Impressionist technique does little to detract from his ability to convey this new bond.

A number of other social factors lie behind the surface of this painting. In the South, emancipation of the slaves inaugurated the economically limiting system of share cropping, which bound the rural poor – black and white alike – to a life of unremitting and costly toil. The upsurge of industry in the North East, spurred on by the demands of the new machine, created large centers of urban population: mouths which had to be fed.

Lastly, in the three decades which followed the war, over 12 million immigrants arrived (causing the national population to double every 27 years), placing even greater pressure on the land already under the plough. But, in spite of these demands, or possibly in response to them, a strong feeling of community was to arise in the agricultural settlements which sprang up in the wake of the westward-moving Frontier □

Romantic Vision

The romanticism that began with Washington Allston in such works as *Moonlit Landscape* (1819) continued through the century and is evidenced in the paintings of Albert Pinkham Ryder (1847–1917), although in many ways Ryder's work is much closer to twentieth-century concepts in art. He visited Europe several times, but unlike most American artists he did not study in the academies of Düsseldorf, Paris or London; apart from some lessons from the romantic painter William E. Marshall he seems to have been largely self-taught.

His method of painting makes the dating of his canvases difficult since he worked and reworked them over a long time-span, building up layer upon layer of pigment and varnishing each one. (This process, and the incorporation of bitumen, caused extensive discoloration with the passage of time and transformed his work so that what we now see is not what Ryder intended.) His ideas evolved very slowly and he often carried the theme of a painting in his mind for several years before committing it to canvas.

Ryder was the archetypal romantic artist working in a garret – a walk-up tenement in New York City – though he was not a complete recluse and had close friends in the art world. Along with Hunt, LaFarge and Saint Gaudens, Ryder founded the Society of American Artists and exhibited his paintings at their annual shows. His earliest work is mainly of landscapes which are reminiscent of the Barbizon School in France, but in the 1880s themes from Shakespeare, the Bible or Wagner – such as *The Flying Dutchman* (1887) – occupied him. In this painting the forms of the waves and the threatening clouds with their anthropomorphic echoes are strongly evocative. The swirling vortex of forms which also appears in other paintings by Ryder reminds us of the late work of Turner, but the surface is more sensuous and is built up almost in three-dimensional pattern, strengthening the links with twentieth-century expressionism. For Ryder the 'natural' forms used in his paintings were but a means of realizing his inner feelings. The shapes and forms that he employed are limited, especially in the sea paintings with a single boat adrift under a cloud-filled sky. This limiting of himself to a few elements and exploring the endless possibilities inherent in them is a concept that occurs often in twentieth-century non-figurative or abstract art.

Like Ryder, Ralph Albert Blakelock (1847–1919) used a limited range of forms in his paintings, which were romantic recollections rather than studies from nature. His images usually consisted of dark foreground trees silhouetted against a light sky with the occasional incorporation of an Indian encampment. *Moonlight, Indian Encampment* (1885–89) is a typical example of this type. Unlike Ryder, however, Blakelock used his limited repertoire of forms to create a lyrical nostalgic image. In this painting two large masses of trees balance either side of the foreground with a misty landscape stretching away into the distance, its color and tone linking it to the sky. The inclusion of the Indian encampment recalls the similar use made of this element in the work of Trumbull at the beginning of the nineteenth century and in Bierstadt's *Rocky Mountains, Lander's Peak* of 1863; it is that of the noble savage in the untouched wilderness. For Blakelock these images are memories of his travels in the West between 1869 and 1872 though by this time, the late 1880s, the image is even more remote from actuality.

Blakelock's personal life was tragic; unable to cope with the burdens imposed by his large family, and exploited by art dealers, he finally succumbed to the strain and entered an asylum in 1899 where he spent the next seventeen years. During this period of isolation his reputation grew and he was elected a member of the National Academy of Design on his release in 1916. However the pressures were still too great for him and he re-entered the asylum in 1918 and died the following year.

Blakelock also reworked his canvases and used bitumen, which has resulted in a deterioration of the surfaces; however, there is still a mystical sense in the light seen through the dark foreground foliage.

The limited formats used by both Ryder and Blakelock attracted the attention of forgers and it is often difficult to authenticate their works.

Throughout the whole of the post-Civil War period European, and specifically French, influences continued to affect the attitudes of American painters in varying degrees. In France, the nineteenth century saw a move away from realism which began in the work of

Albert Pinkham Ryder
Flying Dutchman c. 1887
14¼″ × 17¼″
National Museum of American Art, Smithsonian Institution

A lbert Pinkham Ryder remains a genuine oddity: an artist of
prodigious talent, born too late to be classed with the
Romantics, he was closer in spirit to some of the hot-house hybrids
of European symbolism, in that his work deals with the external
manifestations of psychological extremes – indeed his paintings
presage the psychodramas of Surrealism – while his style verged
upon Abstract Expressionism in its manipulation of pure color and
sublimation of form to distorted notation.

His work is most closely comparable to his French contemporary
Odilon Redon's; in atmosphere he is close to his forebear and
compatriot Edgar Allan Poe. These two points of comparative
reference form a neat circle, in that Poe's work was immensely

popular in France from the late 1840s onwards, and Redon
produced three series of lithographs directly inspired by the works of
the American writer. These often hint at obscure dream landscapes,
but rarely give them the kind of threatening flesh which Ryder could
whip up in paint. This painting could be an illustration to Poe's
Descent Into Maelström *or the* Narrative of Arthur
Gordon Pym □

the neo-classicists such as Jacques Louis David and Jean Auguste Dominique Ingres in the early part of the century and reached naturalism at its most extreme in the paintings of the Impressionists towards the latter end. Romanticists such as Delacroix and Géricault reacted against realism and this in turn influenced the Barbizon group of artists, who were important in promoting the validity of painting directly from the motif, out of doors. Although some artists before this time had painted in the open air they had generally considered these works as preliminary studies for producing 'finished' studio paintings, whereas the Barbizon group led by Corot, Millet, Rousseau and Daubigny acknowledged their *plein air* studies as finished paintings. The painterliness of the

O *ne important aspect of European symbolism was the recycling*
of historical myth in a new, psychologically ambiguous guise.
The paintings of Ralph Blakelock form an American parallel to
this process, but where the European symbolists had centuries of
literary and symbolic accretion with which to play, the Americans
could only fall back on their most immediate myth – that of the
Romantic landscape, first imaged by Washington Allston, and its
inhabitants, the Indians or the early European Settlers.

The better to exploit this limited format, Blakelock introduced
psychological atmospherics (here in the eerie play of moon, light and
dark shadow) and a kind of off-the-shelf nostalgia not dissimilar to
that first used by Claude Lorraine, only here Blakelock has replaced
Arcadians with Red Indians. But at the heart of this painting, the
American Romantic myth remains intact – the indistinct distant
vista across the river is bright with promise □

Romanticists in the use of freer handling combined with the attitudes of the Barbizon group and led ultimately to Impressionism – a concern with recording the transient nature of light – which was to change the course of French art.

American Impressionism

We have seen how the style of the Barbizon painters affected some of the work of American artists but so far all the European influences had been tempered by something specifically American – the retention of the materialism of the object portrayed. It was Impressionism that had the most obvious effect on a group of artists in the United States.

Ralph Albert Blakelock
Moonlight, Indian Encampment c. 1885–88
17⅛″ × 24⅛″
National Museum of American Art, Smithsonian Institution

Several artists such as Winslow Homer, Thomas Eakins and Eastman Johnson showed some influences of this movement but other artists absorbed the lessons much more fully and formed a group of American Impressionists. However the adoption of ideas of Impressionism by these American artists, while producing some significant works in the field of American landscape painting, did not, as in France, completely change the mainstream of art which in the United States retained its strong grasp of realism.

The essence of Impressionism was to take as the subject of the painting not the objects portrayed, whether a landscape, a railway station or a street scene, but to attempt to record the fleeting effects of light, color and atmosphere. In the process of recording light the French Impressionists eliminated black from their palette and relied on primary and secondary colors, plus white. These colors were applied directly to the canvas in unmodified strokes, with the intention that they fuse when seen at a distance to achieve the desired image. Many modifications of this basic aim evolved. Some artists added black, some mixed their colors before applying them to the canvas, some composed their paintings as meticulously as previous artists, but a common aim was the recording of what was seen rather than what was known about the artists' environment.

American Impressionism did not have the same sense of 'a group' that arose in Paris in the nineteenth century, probably because in America the academies did not have the power that they had in France and indeed throughout Europe. The reason for this was that the European academies were formed under Royal or State patronage and consequently recognition of his worth by these academies was one of the supreme aims of the European artist; American academies, however, were formed by individuals and conflict with them was the conflict of individuals rather than the concept of the individual against the state.

George Inness (1825–94) was in his later years hailed as the supreme American landscapist. His early work was firmly grounded in the Hudson River School tradition and after a visit to Paris in 1854 it showed the absorption of elements of the landscape tradition of Claude Lorraine and of the romantic naturalism of the Barbizon School. We saw the effects of these stimuli in his painting *Autumn Meadows* (1869) but in his later paintings such as *Niagara* (1889) the change is dramatic. His initial reaction to the work of the French Impressionists was unfavorable, criticizing Claude Monet and his colleagues for giving art over to purely physical responses, yet *Niagara* and other paintings of this period reveal his aims as being very close to theirs. *Niagara* shows nothing of the romanticism of his earlier Barbizon-influenced paintings but instead a vigorous search for the recording of light and atmosphere. The solutions at which he arrived in this painting place him firmly on the side of the Impressionists although it was an independent development, since he openly despised their attitudes.

These solutions are paralleled by an expatriate American, James McNeill Whistler, who went to Paris in 1855, one year after Inness, studied there for a time and then moved to London, where he spent most of his professional life. The moody landscapes he produced, with the omission of details in favor of a freely painted tonal study, are close to Inness' *Niagara*. Whistler was not the only American to make his fame and fortune outside the United States; Mary Cassatt and John Singer Sargent also spent their lives in Europe and as such fall outside the scope of this book since the landscapes they produced are European.

William Merritt Chase (1849–1916) was one of the artists who absorbed the ideas of the French Impressionists and brought them back to New York. From a visit to Munich he learned a broad, slashing style that derived from the work of Frans Hals and Rubens, but largely abandoned this (although retaining the animated brushwork) in favour of the light palette of Impressionism after meeting Whistler in England. On his return to the United States he taught at various places including the Art Students League, the Brooklyn Art School, the Chicago Art Institute and the Pennsylvania Academy of Design, and also in the open air at Shinnecock, Long Island and at Carmel, California. Eventually he established his own school (which became the New York School of Art). The Shinnecock paintings of the 1880s and the 1890s such as *At the Seaside* (1895) show the French influence in the all-pervading light reducing all forms to patches of color, and the heightened palette is very close to early Monet.

George Inness
Niagara 1889
30″ × 45″
National Museum of American Art, Smithsonian Institution

*T*he thematic options and complexities open to American
landscape painters by the end of the nineteenth century were
fairly broad. We have already seen how various artists took
different lines of approach. In George Inness the American
landscape finally found a painter whose talents could match and
master its natural splendors.

It is notable that his approach was largely formal rather than
thematic; he moved through his early experience of the Hudson
River School, absorbing a broad range of European influences and
ideas from Claude Lorraine up to Monet, and synthesized these in a
remarkable career, which can be compared in its single-minded
pursuit of a formally exact, aesthetically rigid ideal to that of
Turner. It is Inness' immensely informed approach which takes his
work beyond mere naturalism to something more solid and stable, a
style which combines the assurance and structure of classical art
with the close observation of natural effects which characterize
Impressionism□

*T*his beautiful painting, for all its charm and assurance, could
have been painted on either coast of the English Channel, so
steeped is it in the European tradition of late-nineteenth-century
maritime painting. French Impressionism was a great source of
inspiration for William Merritt Chase, tempered with the domestic
lyricism and decorative qualities of English Impressionists such as
Wilson Steer and Sickert. Chase's career reflects that fascination
with Europe among the richer, older families of the North-East
which Henry James describes so exactly in his novels, and it was to

that market that Chase's paintings were designed to appeal. His
proficiency as a painter outweighed his originality, and Chase
remains more notable today as a teacher – among his pupils were
Charles Demuth, Charles Sheeler and Georgia O'Keeffe□

William Merritt Chase
At the Seaside 1895
20″ × 34″
The Metropolitan Museum
of Art

John Henry Twachtman
Round Hill Road c. 1890–
1900
30¼" × 30"
National Museum of
American Art, Smithsonian
Institution

Julian Alden Weir
The Red Bridge 1895
24¼" × 33¾"
The Metropolitan Museum
of Art

Chase's paintings met with considerable success and, as a result of his teaching, his influence was widespread. However the adoption of Impressionism by American artists was not always financially rewarding. Many collectors who became interested in Impressionism wanted to collect French examples rather than native American ones. In addition, many of the newly wealthy Americans looked towards Europe for suitable status symbols to uphold their new position and Old Masters filled this need in preference to American paintings. Nevertheless, in the 1870s many new galleries were established by dealers who were receptive to new ideas and by the 1880s there was a constant dialogue between French and American artists as the Americans travelled back and forth.

Theodore Robinson (1852–96) was one of those who visited Claude Monet, staying with him at Giverny in 1888 and benefiting greatly from his direction. However, he still retained an interest in three-dimensional form though his late works such as *The Red House* (1892) or *Port Ben, Delaware and Hudson Canal* (1893) became looser and more assured. Although he died tragically young and, indeed, spent most of his painting life in Europe, he made a considerable contribution to American landscape painting.

John Henry Twachtman (1853–1902), after some early training in Cincinnati, joined Chase in Venice in 1877. On his return to the United States in 1886 his work was very much in the Barbizon manner, with a heightened palette from his contact with Impressionism. Shortly afterwards he moved to Greenwich, Connecticut, where he bought a farmhouse, and from this time on his work became more Impressionist. (This farmhouse, plus an adjoining farm occupied by J. Alden Weir, formed the nucleus of an American Impressionist colony of which Theodore Robinson was a frequent guest.) Like Monet, Twachtman often painted the same scene again and again. He had a predilection for snow scenes and in these his palette was restricted to subtle variations within a narrow range of colors, as in *Round Hill Road* (c. 1890–1900), which is reminiscent of Monet's

J. *Alden Weir was a leading light among 'the Ten', which represented one of the first organized groups of artists to dissent from the formal body of American academic art teaching. They were, in fact, reconstructing in America the kind of steps taken by the Realists and early Impressionists in Paris in the Salons des Refusés of the 1860s. Thus, 'the Ten' naturally took Impressionism in its most contemporary form as a stylistic starting point. The other significant members of the group were Theodore Robinson, John Henry Twachtman and Childe Hassam.*

Here Weir has deliberately exaggerated the direct impact of Japanese prints (and their indirect impact through the work of Monet, Degas and the Nabis group), to create an eye-catching treatment of landscape in decoratively flattened places and colors. Where it differs from, say, the work of a more doctrinaire Impressionist such as Chase, is in the conscious development of the style away from realistic representation towards a reduction of the pictorial elements to a synthetic harmony, not dissimilar in its effect to the work of Cézanne. The work of 'the Ten' (Chase joined the group when Twachtman died) was to inaugurate a fresh intellectual debate about the aims and methods of painting in the USA □

views of the river Seine in winter (Twachtman exhibited with Monet in New York). In this painting Twachtman flattens space to achieve a lyrical visual poetry.

Ten American Painters

In 1895 several painters from New York and Boston formed themselves into a group – an academy of American Impressionists – under the name the Ten American Painters. Robinson, Twachtman (replaced at his death by Chase), J. Alden Weir and Childe Hassam were the major painters of this group.

The painting of Julian Alden Weir (1852–1919) is close to Twachtman's in its overall mood but is more specific in topography – as in, for example, his *Red Bridge* (1895). There is a strong feeling for decorative picture-making in this work, with its echoes of Japanese design (a feature that is also seen in some of Twachtman's work). Weir came from a family of painters; his father taught drawing at West Point and his brother John F. Weir came to Impressionism through the teaching of William Merritt Chase, who introduced him to the work of Monet. In Weir's work the strong sense of design goes beyond representational Impressionism; it is a much more subjective approach than that of the other members of this group and reflects a personal vision.

The work of Childe Hassam (1859–1935), the other leading member of the Ten, most

Childe Hassam
Late Afternoon, New York:
Winter 1900
37″ × 29″
The Brooklyn Museum

Childe Hassam
Winter in Union Square
Early 1890s
18¼″ × 18″
The Metropolitan Museum
of Art

*T*he architectural embellishment of the great East Coast cities really got under way in the last three decades of the nineteenth century, when the creative genius of the architect H. H. Richardson, and the exploration of new techniques of building by the Chicago School, began to transform the skylines of American cities, which have remained their most outstanding and famous characteristics ever since. The enormous growth in the American economy and population during this period made possible construction and urban growth on an unparalleled scale. Landscape painters were not slow to recognize the importance of this process, and notable among them was Childe Hassam, a co-founder of 'the Ten'. Hassam's views of American urban life at the turn of the century bring to mind those of Renoir, Degas and Pissarro in their fascination with the bustle and movement of street life in a large city, played off against a rich array of atmospheric effects and weather conditions □

closely resembled French Impressionism, with its flickering effects of broken brushwork and scenes of city life; *Winter in Union Square* very closely approximates the street scenes of Paris by Camille Pissarro. Like many early American painters Hassam started his career in the world of art as a printer, becoming an experienced lithographer and etcher with work in magazines such as *Harper's Weekly* and *Century*. During his second trip to Paris in 1886 Hassam decided to become a painter, enrolling at the Académie Julian to study figure drawing, but he also began to paint Parisian street scenes. These ideas persisted in his work after his return to New York in 1889 – a New York which had already seen Durand Ruel's large French Impressionist exhibition and had accepted its ideas. His winter scenes, such as *Winter in Union Square* and *Late Afternoon, New York: Winter* of 1900, exploit the effects of snow to give an overall tonal effect like Twachtman's, softening harsh outlines and dissolving forms.

Ruel Brings Impressionism to America

The year of 1886 was an important one for American Impressionists. The French art dealer, Paul Durand Ruel, held the first large exhibition in New York of paintings by Barbizon School and French Impressionist artists and, as a result of this, Impressionism was raised in status in America and was recognized by the National Academy of Design. However, it could be said that recognition brought its downfall as it became but a new academic mode in the same way that it was absorbed by the Royal Academy in England and academies in Europe. By 1892 the acceptance of Impressionism as the official academic doctrine had completely taken over the Society of American Artists. This society had been established by younger artists to counteract the academicism of the National Academy of Design and it had attracted the greatest painters of its generation including Thomas Eakins, who joined it in 1880 – but in 1892 it was the Society of American Artists who rejected Eakins' *The Agnew Clinic* because of its stark, uncompromising realism. The avant-garde had become the academic.

In France reaction to Impressionism came from within the group and developed in diverse directions with the expressionist turmoil of Vincent Van Gogh, the symbolism of Gauguin, the intellectual structural concepts of Cézanne and the quasi-scientific use of optics of Seurat. These painters were collectively known as the post-Impressionists.

American artists, though influenced in varying degrees by the ideas of the French Impressionists, were unaware, or unaffected by, the French post-Impressionist developments. In the last years of the nineteenth century American art degenerated into a smug complacency dominated by the academy – which in turn was dominated by the Ten.

Ash Can School

This was a period of abundance in the United States and machine production, based on the industrial organization of Henry Ford's mass production techniques, was seen as the panacea for social problems. This phenomenon affected American culture in many ways, the significant one in the visual arts being the growth of newpapers and the illustrative processes used in them. The main reaction to the academy came from a group of artists of whom most had started in Philadelphia as newspaper illustrators, and it was the boom in newspaper production coupled with new methods of reproducing images in the press that brought the work of Henri, Luks, Glackens, Sloan and Shinn to the public.

The leader of the group was Robert Henri (1865–1929), the son of a real estate investor by the name of Cozad who was also a professional gambler. After a gambling fight Cozad left the Nebraska town named after him and changed his name to Richard Lee and his sons' names to Robert Henri and Frank Southrn. Henri studied at the Pennsylvania Academy and in France, financed by his father. Here he was exposed to the French Impressionists and reacted against them. On his return from Europe to Philadelphia, Henri found a group of sympathetic companions in John Sloan, William Glackens, George Luks and Everett Shinn. He persuaded them that the American scene, with its energy and diversity, was a worthy subject for their painting. Henri was the leading political force in this group and his radicalism was not confined solely to the art field; he was a liberal reformer and a constant crusader against inequality in the social system, maintaining a strong belief that all tradition was a stumbling block to progress and justice.

Robert Henri
Snow in New York 1902
32″ × 25¾″
National Gallery of Art,
Washington DC; Chester
Dale Collection

*T*he urban experience of America was for many their principal encounter with the American landscape. As usual, real wealth and opportunity resided in the large cities, and over one third of the US population lived in the crowded cities of the North and North-East – Milwaukee, Chicago, Detroit, Cleveland, Buffalo, Boston, Pittsburgh, New York, Philadelphia, Cincinnati, Baltimore and New York, contained over 11 million people between them. On the one hand the urban growth of the United States was the phenomenon of the age, on the other, it contained the virulent baccili of urban decay – tenements, ghettos, organized crime and urban discontent.

Many of the Realists of the first decade of the twentieth century accurately identified the paradoxical status of these vast cities.

Wonders of engineering, architecture and town planning, the playrooms of the socially sophisticated, they were nevertheless, at street level, desolate canyons perched on the first circle of Hell for the poor and underprivileged. Some of the paintings of Robert Henri convey this ambiguous status, his proto-Expressionist brushwork drawing the brownstone gloom down to the sidewalks and gutters of these mean streets □

To modern eyes the art produced by these men does not appear radical but a natural development of the American school of realism, handed down from Eakins to his pupil at the Pennsylvania Academy, Thomas Anshutz, and in turn to the latter's disciple, Robert Henri. However, it was a realism tempered by their common ground as newspaper reporters – the forerunner of today's photojournalists. Henri and Luks worked for the *Bulletin*, Glackens for the *Record*, the *Public Ledger* and the *Press*, Sloan for the *Press*, and Shinn for five different newspapers.

From 1895 members of this group began to move to New York, where they each took jobs in the press and also turned to painting as opposed to newspaper illustration. Henri took a post in 1903 as a teacher at the New York School of Art – founded by Chase – and taught there for four years until disagreement with Chase persuaded him to open his own school. After five years there he moved on to the Art Students' League.

It was through his teaching that Henri was most influential. In addition to being the driving force behind the Philadelphia group he had a considerable influence on George Bellows, who came to study with him at the New York School of Art in 1904, and on a whole generation which included Rockwell Kent, Glenn Coleman and Edward Hopper.

Ash Can Revolt

The basic tenets of the group that Henri formed – which was to become known as the Ash Can School – was the search for and depiction of 'truth' as opposed to beauty. The Ash Can School was a revolt against the genteel images which were produced by their predecessors, especially the 'Ten'. In their place they looked for truth in crudity and ugliness, particularly in the slum life of big cities. These cities had grown at an explosive rate in the 1880s and 1890s and with the industrial expansion had come an increase in immigration from Europe. These newcomers settled in the slum areas of the cities and retained their ethnic culture. The social problems were great at this time, and these included the exploitation of immigrant and child labor in the sweat shops of the inner cities. This milieu of slum life with its variety of cultures formed the subject matter for Henri and his comrades, each of whom formed his own personal vision of this world.

On Henri's return from Europe he had turned to the darker side of the palette and it was this palette with his choice of street scenes such as *Snow in New York* (1902) that laid the foundation for the remainder of the group – most of whom would have remained as illustrative journalists without Henri's teaching. As the theoretician for the Ash Can School Henri proposed the realism of Eakins in his book *The Art Spirit*. He emphasized a break with the dominance of European traditions and with organized art societies, and he aimed to show the value of native American ideas in his proposals for a new democratic art that would reflect the everyday world. Having found the choice of subjects for the group, Henri soon gave up landscapes in favor of dramatic portraits which have the vitality and realism of Manet's paintings and the slashing strokes of Frans Hals.

The closest of the group to Henri was John Sloan (1871–1951), whose interest lay in social reform. Aubrey Beardsley, Art Nouveau and Japanese prints were all important influences in forming his early decorative work but under the tutelage of Henri he abandoned this style and turned to bold, vigorous paintings of beach scenes and cityscapes which have an intimacy which is lacking in Henri's work – an intimacy which is displayed in subjects such as a man releasing pigeons on a rooftop, a woman hanging out washing or children at play in a backyard in Greenwich Village. In all of these his art is full of human interest typified by *Dust Storm, Fifth Avenue* (1906) and it is this warmth that sets Sloan above the rest of the group. John Sloan was 40 before he sold a painting; in New York he taught at the Art Students' League while churning out new versions of his early pictures, since these were the paintings that the dealers wanted.

George Luks (1867–1933) had the very opposite approach to Sloans's warm one. He was an independent, quarrelsome man who spread fantastic stories about his past until he began to believe in them and started to live according to this self-created myth. His work was very close to Henri's, particularly the early work that he painted in Paris in the 1890s. He identified strongly with the lower classes, not merely seeing them as suitable subjects for painting but enjoying the company of the underprivileged, colorful characters he could find in the slums and more especially in the bars where he spent much of his

John Sloan
Dust Storm, Fifth Avenue
1906
22" × 27"
The Metropolitan Museum of Art

*R*obert Henri's fresh and iconoclastic view was to inspire a group of Philadelphia-based artist/illustrator/journalists, among them William Glackens, George Luks, Everett Shinn and John Sloan. The latter was the most inspired of the group, using urban Realism as a starting point for highly individual scenes of city life, drawing on the picturesque qualities of street characters, while retaining their essential vivacity and human spirit. He was capable of seeing the bizarre in big city life, and indeed his characters often seem unnaturally buoyant given their surroundings.

Even here, where Sloan has captured the strange sensation of a dust storm barreling up the man-made canyons of the city, the sense of panic is undercut by his quirky sense of humanity's individuality. Where some of the small children in the center are in a state of real panic, other figures have enough presence of mind to clutch their hats to their heads. There is a metaphysical quality which exposes the heart of Sloan's work – the strong contrast between nature, normal human nature, and the impersonal, abstract setting of the man-made environment of the city □

time. He avoided respectability in all its forms even though he came from a cultured family – his father was a doctor and his mother a painter.

Luks painted the poor not from a feeling of sympathy but because for him the turmoil of slum life had an excitement which his middle-class background lacked. To him the slums were places of adventure, struggle and happiness and not, as they were often perceived, places of dullness and resignation.

The spontaneity of Luks' work resembles most closely Impressionism in its vigorous surface, seen, for example, in *Armistice Night* (1918) but the addition of the darker palette

George Luks
Armistice Night 1918
37″ × 68¾″
Whitney Museum of
American Art, New York

*T*here is a great sense of energy in this painting by Luks, with its swirling flags and the vigorous handling of the figures which make up most of the lower part of the canvas. The diagonal shapes of these flags create a different set of rhythms to the small marks which make up the multitude of people and contrast with the barely discernible geometric skeletons of the skyscrapers in the hazy blue background.

Great use is made of the effects of the artificial light from the street lamps falling on the crowds of people, giving an Impressionist feeling to the painting □

*A*nother follower of Henri was William Glackens, whose experience of French Realism, and of the early works of Manet and Cézanne, when in Paris in the 1890s, served to produce a style which blended his journalist's eye (he worked for the Philadelphia Press *and covered the Spanish-American War in 1898) with a taste for the sophistication of urban life, comparable to similar treatments of Parisian life by Manet, Degas and Renoir. His scenes of the city parks on high days and holidays are among his most popular and successful works. They convey a feeling for city life no less intense, but less gloomy, than those of Henri or Sloan. His light touch declined, after about 1910, into a less critical illustrative style, losing the understated social comment which gave his earlier works their cutting edge □*

William James Glackens
Central Park in Winter
1905
25″ × 30″
The Metropolitan Museum
of Art

and the bold brushwork reminiscent of Frans Hals is also evident in this work.

Robert Henri and William Glackens (1870–1938) went to France in 1895. Glackens had been an artist reporter for the *Philadelphia Ledger* but under the influence of Henri gave it up to devote himself to painting. On his return to America in 1896 he took up another magazine appointment, in New York, and also started exhibiting his work. In 1898, accompanied by George Luks, Glackens went to Cuba to cover the Spanish-American war, and it was as a reporter that his realism was at its strongest. The concerns of the Ash Can School affected his painting for but a short time. His interest in slum life was not, as for other members of the group, a political or social one but was purely concerned with it as a spectacle; he failed to see the poverty or oppression and instead saw the humor and carefree quality. As an artist of means (he married a wealthy student), he was perhaps unable to recognize the struggle for survival in the slums. His handling and use of somber color during his Ash Can phase show the tradition of Manet's work such as *The Funeral* (1870–71). Glackens' painting *Central Park in Winter* (1905) is from this stage,

Unlike the rest of the Ash Can School, Shinn tended to prefer the glitter and glamor of the world of the theater, but this painting of down-and-outs in the city shows his ability to capture the squalor of their predicament. In it he moves away from his fashionable illustrative style to a vigorous calligraphic technique within a bold tonal composition. The depression of the subjects is given greater poignancy in this work by the grandeur of the architectural setting □

before he came under the spell of Impressionism and began to produce works such as *Crowd at the Seashore* (1910), with its more intense colors and broken brushwork. In later canvases, under the influence of Renoir and Impressionism, he threw aside all attempts at realism in favor of sweet, light-filled paintings. Although he retained his interest in realism in his drawings as a reporter his paintings moved into the realm of decorative art.

Although Everett Shinn (1876–1953) is now seen as a minor figure in American art, he was one of the original group of five Philadelphia reporters. His early interest in science involved him in mechanical drafting for a newspaper; from here he moved on to illustration and to the Pennsylvania Academy of Fine Arts. During this time he worked in the orbit of the Ash Can School, painting city life, but became more and more seduced by the theatrical world, painting many figures of the stage and designing sets.

His painting is not as rugged as that of some of the artists of the group and he preferred a fashionable illustrative style, but he could also capture the squalor of the city as is shown in his pastel drawings of down and outs such as *Bums Asleep* (1903). His largest

Everett Shinn
Bums Asleep on the Steps
of the Sub Treasury
Building 1903
8¼″ × 13″
Courtesy of Hirschl & Adler
Galleries Inc., New York

work was a group of murals for the City Hall in Trenton, New Jersey, in which he dropped the rococo manner he had adopted for his theater projects and reverted to his earlier realist style. The importance of these murals is in the depiction of contemporary industrialism in America – the first example of this subject on such a scale – but certain deficiencies of spatial relationships and composition on this large scale prevented the acceptance of the murals as a major step in American art. After this series he returned to the world of the theater as designer and playwright and even became an art director for motion pictures.

The rejection of the work of these five artists by the Academy of Design in 1907 was the stimulus which led them, in company with Arthur B. Davies, Ernest Lawson and Maurice Prendergast, to form the 'Eight' and exhibit their work in 1908 in New York at the Macbeth Gallery. Although the new members were not painting in the same realist style as the 'Five' they were bound by a common rejection of the conservatism of the Academy. The Macbeth Gallery exhibition fulfilled the ideals of Henri – an exhibition of a group of artists with related ideas, organized by themselves with their own choice of work, without the intervention of juries and the attraction of prizes. It was a format used again by the Independent Artists Exhibition in 1910 and the Eight were pivotal in the organization of the Armory Show of 1913. The Macbeth Gallery exhibition was also instrumental in establishing the Eight as a group; it also attracted many derogatory names and this was when the label 'Ash Can School' was first used.

Of the new members of the group, Arthur B. Davies (1862–1928) painted idealist pictures of nudes in dreamlike landscapes and became one of the prime movers of the Armory show of 1913; Ernest Lawson (1873–1939) was a painter of Impressionist landscapes which are much more forceful that those of Twachtman and Hassam, to whom his style is closest. His work goes beyond the surface charm of much American Impressionism and shows a strong underlying structural form such as is found in the work of Paul Cézanne. His exposure to Impressionism came through contact with John Twachtman and J. Alden Weir at their Connecticut colony and with Alfred Sisley, whom he met in Paris in 1893. Lawson's painting *Boathouse, Winter, Harlem River* is a typical example of his strongly structural version of Impressionism. Although he was elected an associate of the National Academy of Design in 1908 he exhibited with the Eight as a protest against the reactionary mentality of the Academy.

The member of the Eight with the most radical style was Maurice B. Prendergast (1859–1924), and he was the only one who evolved an American equivalent of post-

Ernest Lawson
Boathouse, Winter,
Harlem River 1914
40½″ × 50⅛″
Corcoran Gallery of Art

Maurice Prendergast
Central Park 1908–10
20¾″ × 27″
The Metropolitan Museum
of Art

*T*he Philadelphia painters were to be joined, in an exhibition in New York in 1908, by the Symbolist painter Arthur B. Davies, and the Impressionists Maurice Prendergast and Ernest Lawson, in a group which became popularly identified as representing the American avant-garde – known as 'the Eight'. Nearly all of them were aware of, and heavily influenced by, the European art scene, as had been 'the Ten' before them.

But 'the Eight' had turned their diverse talents to dealing with subjects which were uniquely American. Lawson was the least outspoken of 'the Eight', but his delicate style, which showed an awareness of the work of Seurat and the older Pissarro, was the most formally innovative of the group, looking forward to the dissolution of form and of traditional composition of the early Abstract Expressionists.

'The Eight' included a number of diverse talents, and their styles cannot be united under any particular banner other than that of

discontent with traditional academic practice. Such a stance often provokes extremes in both the avant-garde and the establishment groups of protagonists. Maurice Prendergast took various elements of the European avant-garde – Seurat's monumental modernist canvases, Cézanne's reappraisal of color and brushwork, Matisse's reduction of form to simple contours and color planes – and worked toward a new synthesis of form and color resolved by patterning. His urban views are often set in parks, where the tension between the formal procession and the incidental provided a diversity of motifs around which an informal dissolution of paint and color could be arranged □

Impressionism. The style of his work is a decorative surface of patches of color which go beyond the recording of light to form a 'stained glass' effect; it parallels some of the Parisian developments of the post-Impressionists and as a friend of Paul Cézanne he absorbed some of his ideas. We see this style in *Central Park* (c. 1908–10) which was painted before the impact of modernism on American art brought about by the Armory Show. In his day his work was derided for the bold composition and color and it appeals more to modern tastes. Although allied to the group, and exhibiting with Henri and his comrades, his work falls outside the parameters of their realism.

As one of Henri's favorite students it is possible that George Wesley Bellows (1882–1925) would have been invited to exhibit at the Macbeth Gallery with the rest of the

The joys and horrors of big city life were most successfully captured by George Bellows. A camp-follower rather than a member of 'the Eight', his work remains more ambitious and successful than theirs, capturing the reality and diversity of the urban experience. From smoky dives, boxing rings and gambling dens to the crowded bustle of the New York avenues, Bellows work encapsulates those aspects of East Coast city life which have most readily entered the American myth.

His view of the city, specifically New York, is that which forms the backdrop to a whole view of American literary imagery stretching from Dreiser to O'Hara, from the squalor of Sister Carrie *to the glamorous nightlife of* Pal Joey. *The range of his subject was matched by the versatility of his style, at the center of which lay a remarkable ability to capture the essence of movement – on a powerful individual scale as in his famous* Stag at Sharkey's, *or as here, on a panoramic canvas, where innumerable pedestrian figures jostle for attention, while the traffic is, ironically, locked at a standstill* □

Eight in the controversial show of 1908 if he had not been opposed by Sloan, who regarded his work as overly sentimental. Much of Bellows' work reflects the physicality of his interests. As a former prize-fighter he used this subject in *Stag at Sharkeys*, but he also painted many landscapes and scenes from city life such as *New York, February, 1911* (1911), a large painting of the teeming life of the city with its crowds of people, its vehicles and its skyscrapers. It is in these tumultuous cityscapes that Bellows is closest to the spirit of the Ash Can School. Unlike many of his contemporaries he did not study in Europe but learned much from Henri and was to become the youngest elected member of the National Academy.

When compared to some of the earlier Realists Bellows' work lacks the discipline of

George Wesley Bellows
New York, February, 1911
1911
42″ × 60″
National Gallery of Art,
Washington DC

The bitter North American winter was not a subject often painted by the nineteenth-century Romantics – not only did it reveal Nature as a harsh and untrustworthy force, but the reduction of color and form under blanketing snow was not to their taste. The Impressionists and Realists were attracted by exactly those features the Romantics avoided, and certainly for the urban painters such as Henri, snow provided a useful pictorial counterpoint to the dark colors of the city streets.

Rockwell Kent was one of the first pure landscapists to concentrate on the rural winter – attracted by the limited tonal range imposed on his palette, and by the monumental shapes and stark contrasts brought out in the winter landscape. His painting is part of that great thrust towards simplicity and purity of form which runs like a silver thread through progressive art in the opening years of this century, and in his work we begin to see an interest in shape, pigment and tone as elements largely independent of the scene they are being used to capture □

Rockwell Kent
Snow Fields (Winter in the Berkshires) 1909
38″ × 44″
National Museum of
American Art, Smithsonian
Institution

trained draftsmanship but in its stead it has the vitality that he learned from Henri. He executed his paintings very rapidly, occasionally finishing three in one day. His best work was completed before the Armory Show, after which it became stifled by the imposition of artistic theories and superficial 'polish'. The early work has a sense of directness and spontaneity which later became submerged by these other considerations.

Rockwell Kent (1882–1971) was another student of Henri's, although he found his inspiration not in the slums of the city but in the vastness of the northern territories. If figures are included in these paintings they are there to underline the scale of this vast landscape rather than to make any social comment. In the winter Kent would often leave his wife in New York and travel to Alaska or Canada to paint the impressive scenery; paintings such as *Snow Fields* (1909) capture well the atmosphere of the light and the landscape. Although much of his fame depends on the work that he did in the 1930s of popular illustration it is mannered when compared to the fluid, dynamic landscapes of his earlier years.

In spite of the success of the 1908 show in the Macbeth Gallery – sales amounted to nearly $4,000 and the show was circulated through eight cities by the Pennsylvania Academy – the grouping of the Eight was not repeated. Perhaps its impact was in reviving organized opposition to the stranglehold of the Academy and in triggering the Exhibition of Independent Artists of 1910 which included the Eight and their followers and prepared the New York art world for new ideas. However, the arrival of the Armory Show in 1913 with its ideas of 'modernism' soon overshadowed the accomplishments of the Ash Can School. Although the most significant work produced by this group dates from after 1900 the philosophy and style is much closer to nineteenth-century ideas than to the modernism of twentieth-century painting and thus qualifies it for inclusion in this chapter.

Folk Art

The art of the naive or folk artist continues to occupy a special place in the story of American landscape painting. Untrained painters with a childlike vision are found in all cultures, but in the United States they have attained an exalted status. Perhaps this is connected with the brevity of American culture in relation to that of Europe and elsewhere, or it may be because it is an extension of the limner tradition – a style established as a decorative craft used in the making of signs and the production of painted overmantels and wall panels. This style derived from the linear traditions of England in the fifteenth and sixteenth century and from early Dutch art, but in its American adaptation it was a style strongly associated with the early immigrants and with rural life. For Americans it has a strong nostalgia value, since all Americans apart from American Indians are either immigrants or descendants of immigrants. In its simplicity and obvious naive quality it evokes images (admittedly romanticized ones) of a less cluttered age with a simpler life style.

Although many of the folk artists, particularly before the mid-nineteenth century, were either anonymous figures or were known only within a small provincial group, Edward Hicks (1780–1849) was very widely renowned. He was not only a painter but also a Quaker preacher in which capacity he traveled widely, spreading the word of God to the Friends' meetings. At the age of 13 he had been apprenticed to a coachmaker and, as an adult, he began to decorate household objects and subsequently trade signboards to produce extra income above what he earned from his coach work.

The conventions that he acquired through these crafts continued in his later paintings, which are characterized by a bold linear outline style, the use of lettered subtitles and the decorative borders which surround such paintings as *The Falls of Niagara* (1825). His most famous works are the series of paintings of the *Peaceable Kingdom*, illustrating Isaiah's prophecy of a world at peace under God, which date from 1820 onwards. About 60 versions of this subject survive. Hicks also produced several views of the residences of gentlemen which, like his many versions of the *Peaceable Kingdom*, bear witness to his love of painting animals. These canvases act as a visual record of the wealth and prestige of the farmer by depicting all his worldly goods. *Cornell Farm* (1848) shows the owner's prize-winning bull and farm stock with the farm stretching away into the distance.

Edward Hicks
The Cornell Farm 1848
36¾″ × 49″
National Gallery of Art,
Washington DC

In the search for a means of achieving pictorial simplicity, artists in Europe and America were drawn to various disparate sources for ideas and inspiration: 'primitive' art was foremost among them, and African, Oceanic and American Indian art began to be highly valued and widely collected. Another primary source was the work of naive painters; in France, Le Douanier Rousseau and Louis Vivin enjoyed growing reputations. In America, a long tradition of naive folk painting came to be regarded in a new and much more favorable light.

The work of the early nineteenth-century Quaker preacher and painter Hicks is a particularly fine example of the tradition; his technique was in fact quite sophisticated, and he displayed a strong feeling for form and detail. From an historical viewpoint his work remains a more accurate and telling record of life in the North-East than the paintings of, for example, the Hudson River School.

His primary aim was to provide an accurate visual record of his subject, although like the painters of the Hudson River School, his work moves beyond the outward appearance of things in an attempt to convey a spiritual (in this case Christian) presence in the world about him □

Although the work of Hicks has great force and vitality and is far superior to that of most of his folk artist contemporaries he himself underrated the quality of his painting and saw himself primarily as a preacher.

One of the salient features of folk art is its timeless quality; the work of the early nineteenth century is often close to that of an artist a hundred years later. An example of this is the painting *Manchester Valley* by Joseph Pickett (1848–1918) which, until the life of the artist was researched, was exhibited as dating from the early nineteenth century. It was actually painted during the period of the First World War between 1914–18. Trained as a carpenter under his father, who had moved to New Hope, Pennsylvania, in 1840 to work on the canal locks, Pickett made his living from carpentry and from a country store selling groceries and general goods, starting to paint in his spare time at around the age of 42. Like Hicks, Pickett never really considered his painting as anything but a pastime and it was not until the last year of his life that he sent a painting to the annual exhibition at the Pennsylvania Academy of Fine Arts – where he received three votes, including that of Robert Henri. It was only in the 1930s, when his work was included in the large exhibition of folk art at the Museum of Modern Art, New York, and the Newark Museum, that his painting was truly recognized.

The technique that he used in his painting was unique in its mixing of sand with house paints to build up low relief textured surfaces, and he later progressed to using artists' oil paints in the same way. The painting *Manchester Valley* was executed to commemorate the coming of the railroad to New Hope and reflects the changing landscape of America brought about by industry and the new forms of transport. It displays much that is typical of folk art, including the artist's attitude of seeing things conceptually rather than according to a logical linear perspective.

Unlike Hicks' *Cornell Farm*, which has a convincing sense of space and a logical, if somewhat exaggerated, form of perspective, *Manchester Valley* ignores scale and distance and stacks up buildings and other objects in a vertical fashion across the surface of the painting, emphasizing everything equally. With this childlike style, Pickett's combinations of color and inventive pattern produce images of great vitality.

Like many American artists John Kane (1860–1934) was a recent immigrant, moving to the United States at the age of nineteen from Scotland – and like many American artists he started painting late in life. He worked as a laborer on all kinds of jobs – on the railroad, in mining, and house painting – and was one of the multitude of unskilled and

John Kane
From My Studio Window
1932
22⅜″ × 34⅜″
The Metropolitan Museum
of Art

Joseph Pickett
Manchester Valley
1914–18? Oil with sand on
canvas
45½″ × 60⅝″
Museum of Modern Art, New
York. Gift of Abby Aldrich
Rockefeller

*W*here Hicks earned much of his living from painting furniture, houses, signboards and rich farmers, Joseph Pickett was a genuine amateur, a true Sunday painter. Like many folk artists, Pickett shows an unnerving ability to make a telling choice of subject matter and to bring his paintings to life with a great intensity of vision.

His work on the whole rejects strict observation of nature in favor of an ideal, simplified and decorative view of the American landscape in which all is neat and ordered, everything has its place and function. Like that of Hicks, Pickett's work provides, despite its quirky approach, a particularly accurate record of the sort of everyday life and events usually overlooked by 'serious' artists.

John Kane's work is more knowing than that of Pickett, probably as a result of Kane's broad experience of the laboring, outdoor life, indeed his biography reads like that of a folk-hero: Scottish immigrant, railroad worker, construction laborer, prize-fighter. His meticulous paintings, produced late in life, detail his life and become, in a sense, a homage to the industrial worker's lot. In this they bear a resemblance to the folk songs of Leadbelly and Woody Guthrie, but with little of the active protest voiced in their work.

Again, Kane displays considerable sophistication for a self-

taught painter: his handling of color is rudely harmonious, his rendering of space and recession is convincing, and his eye for just the right detail to draw the viewer into the implicit narrative of his paintings is particularly finely-judged □

semi-skilled workers employed in the developing industrial sector of America. He loved to box and his pride in his physique is apparent in a half-length self portrait painted in 1929 when he was 69 years old which shows his still-muscular body in a frontal pose like a fighter. Following an accident on the railroad in 1891 in which he lost a leg, he became a watchman and then started painting railroad cars. It was here that his landscape interest was kindled and he executed scenes on the cars in his lunchbreak, painting over them when he returned to work. When this job came to an end he began to enlarge and hand color photographs to support his growing family.

Tragedy was again present in his life when he lost his only son at just a day old. Thereupon he turned to drink, separated from his family and continued his wandering

The outstanding American naive or folk painter of this century remains Grandma Moses, whose long career, enormous range of pictorial invention, and detailed evocation of New England country life resulted in a great number of paintings, and great popularity.

The strength of her imagery was twofold: firstly she drew on her own personal memories for the look and activities of the landscape, providing the public with an historical view of the landscape, which, being at most only two or three generations removed from that of her contemporaries, remained comfortable and accessible. Secondly, she fed her extraordinary imagination with a supply of received or 'found' material – images from photographs, postcards and magazine illustrations which gave variety to her paintings, while guaranteeing a feeling of shared, familiar nostalgia. The overall effect was enhanced by her polished, child-like style, which contributed to the aura of innocence as well as being immediately identifiable □

life, earning money from carpentry and house painting. During these wanderings he began painting landscapes on scraps of wood. It was in 1927 that Kane received recognition at the age of 67 when a painting was accepted by the Carnegie Institute International Exhibition and this was followed by further exhibitions in both Pittsburgh and New York. From this time on his work was eagerly sought by several major collectors.

Details and the structure of objects play an important role in his painting, probably as a result of the many manual trades that he pursued during his lifetime; *From My Studio Window* (1932) is a typical example of his attention to minutiae. Throughout his painting career he found inspiration in the industrial age – the cities, factories and railroads.

Grandma Moses
Hoosick Falls in Winter
1944
19¾″ × 23¾″
The Phillips Collection,
Washington DC

*T*he vertical viewpoint and the linear emphasis and stylization
of forms allies this work by Wood to the conceptual folk
tradition although there is a sophistication in the handling of this
viewpoint which one does not find in folk art. The stylization of the
rounded trees and the rounded shapes of the hills with the road
following the curves gives a linear rhythmical quality to the whole
painting. Against the tortuous winding lines the strong vertical of
the church spire combined with the chimney of the house directly
below it on the canvas provide a strong stabilizing element. Even the
light in this painting is stylized and adds to the overall pattern □

Of all the folk artists in America the most well-known of the twentieth century is certainly Grandma Moses – Anna May Robertson Moses (1860–1961). She was also the most successful within her lifetime and her work was reproduced on greetings cards and calendars and in prints. As with many folk artists, her career as a painter started late in life at the age of 67 but she continued painting until her death at the age of 101, so her active painting life still spanned over 34 years.

Her subjects are based on the New England countryside and evoke a strong mood of nostalgia. Many of her early paintings are copies of, or use sections from, prints by Currier and Ives from artists such as George Henry Durrie which she then recomposed in her own way. In her versions the figures became more stylized and the landscapes less naturalistic. Her painting was preceded by the production of landscapes in needlework and it was only the onset of arthritis that forced the change of medium. The images, however, continued the same and she re-executed some of her needlework landscapes in paint at a later date.

From these early sources she then began to compose original paintings such as *Hoosick Falls, New York in Winter* (1944) which relied on her surroundings and her memories of country life and activities; these paintings display an increasing technical ability. By the 1940s her work had become a marketable commodity and collectors created a demand for her paintings; by the end of the decade she had become a national celebrity, appearing on radio and television.

Like many painters of the nineteenth and twentieth centuries Grandma Moses made use of photographs for information, for figures, for fragments of landscape and for buildings, but her work, especially that of her later years, was not a slavish copying of these but compositions using them as source material. Her output was prodigious and consequently her work is of varying quality but though her public appeal is based as much on the emotive image of the 'Grandma' figure producing naive pictures of country life as on her actual paintings, she ranks among the top folk painters of the nineteenth and twentieth centuries.

The folk art tradition has often been close to the mainstream of artistic developments. The linearity and clarity in some of the Luminist paintings, such as the work of Kensett and Lane for example, can be seen as reflecting this tradition. There is also the conceptual nature of much American art which appears as one of the most characteristic features of folk art landscapes. Even when the painting is produced in front of the subject two viewpoints are used – the objects in the landscape are painted as though seen from ground level, but the disposition of them on the painted surface is in the form of a map as though seen from above. This conceptual approach is seen in many artists' work and the inclusion of Grant Wood (1892–1942) in this section illustrates the persistence of this tradition.

With Thomas Hart Benton and John Steuart Curry, Grant Wood was one of the foremost Regionalists of the 1930s – a group of artists who rejected European influences of Modernism and turned inwards to the heartland of America for their subjects. Benton's and Curry's work are discussed and illustrated in the following chapter – Coming of Age in America – on pages 124–29, and Grant Wood's contribution could just as easily have been included in that section.

In spite of their aversion to acknowledging any debt to European sources all three Regionalists had visited Europe. Wood went to Germany in 1928 and the impact of the Flemish and German artists' use of glazes and clearly defined images is reflected in his own style. *The Midnight Ride of Paul Revere* (1931) shows this linearity which was also a characteristic of the early American limners and the Luminists but here is combined with a bird's eye view. The whole approach of the painting is conceptual, with the undulating stylized landscape, the 'lollipop' trees and the clearcut buildings, all of which ally it to some extent with the folk tradition.

Grant Wood's images have a sophistication and a technical expertise that many folk artists lack, but the similarities are still evident and show the persistence of certain attitudes. Indeed, the influence of folk art is visible throughout much of American realist painting from the Luminists of the nineteenth century to the Precisionists of the twentieth.

Grant Wood
The Midnight Ride of Paul Revere 1931
30″ × 40″
The Metropolitan Museum of Art

COMING OF AGE
IN AMERICA

February 17, 1913 – the date of the Armory Show in New York – serves as a convenient starting point for twentieth-century ideas in American art.

The Armory Show (held in the 69th Regiment Armory in New York) brought, among other things, the new ideas of Modernism which came from Europe to the attention of the American public. However, for a small artistic elite of painters and collectors these ideas were already familiar. Alfred Stieglitz, perhaps best known as a photographer, was very influential in importing Modernist ideas to America. In 1905 he opened the Photo-Secession Gallery, also known as 291, initially to promote new ideas in photography but then extending it to embrace all new ideas in art.

Drawings by Rodin was one of the major exhibitions at this gallery in 1908, followed by drawings by Matisse. Rodin's fame as a sculptor cajoled the critics into accepting his drawings but the work of Matisse, although deriving from similar ideas, was attacked. This established Stieglitz's position as a defender of the avant-garde in art and produced exhibitions of works by John Marin, Max Weber, Paul Cézanne, Toulouse Lautrec and Picasso – in fact all the significant figures in Modernism, both European and American. Whereas Robert Henri in the early years of the twentieth century had proposed a democratic art – an art for the people – Stieglitz and his circle saw mass reproduction of art works and mass education in art as a degenerating influence; art for them was exclusive – by the few for the few. Stieglitz remained the patriarch of the circle which gathered at 291 and lasted until the onset of World War I.

The Armory Show – or the International Exhibition of Modern Art – brought to a wider audience much of the work that Stieglitz had been championing at 291. Its origin was in the formation of the Association of American Painters and Sculptors by a group of 25 established artists in New York in 1911 who were dissatisfied with the National Academy of Design. Their purpose was to hold exhibitions of the best contemporary art in both America and Europe. Under the control of the Eight – the Ash Can School – the Association's primary purpose was going to be to promote the recent art of Americans with the hope of improving its patronage. Most art buyers still looked to European old masters and ignored local talent. However, the inclusion of Arthur B. Davies as its President expanded the nationalism of the original proposal to include progressive European art.

The exhibition was a mammoth undertaking, with approximately 1600 pieces of art

Arthur Dove
City Moon 1938
34⅞″ × 25″
Hirshhorn Museum and
Sculpture Garden,
Smithsonian Institution

organized in historical sequence to show the development of ideas in art and the gradual acceptance of revolutionary forms. The European part of the show traced developments through nineteenth-century French painting from Ingres through the Romanticists to Impressionism and post-Impressionism. Bonnard and Vuillard, the Fauves – Matisse, Derain, Vlaminck – and the Cubists – Picasso, Braque, Duchamp, Léger – were all represented. The idea of demonstrating an evolutionary process in art did not convince the spectators at the exhibition, which drew an unprecedented press coverage. The work of Matisse produced an uproar while the Cubist paintings, especially Marcel Duchamp's *Nude Descending a Staircase*, became the main targets for criticism. Cubism was a style developed in Paris simultaneously by Picasso and Braque in which the aims of Cézanne were taken further. The latter had tried to go beyond the mere surface of objects which was the preoccupation of Impressionism and explore the solidity of form of the objects portrayed while not destroying the integrity of the two dimensional surface of the canvas. Cubism showed a concern with form and color and the interaction of the picture surface with the analysis of form. This often resulted in combinations of multiple viewpoints of the object, expressing its totality rather than just one aspect of it.

The Armory Show became a kind of circus sideshow, much as art exhibitions had been promoted in the early nineteenth century, though this time it was unintentional. Nevertheless, in spite of the critics and of the ridicule leveled at some of the exhibits, the show was a great success with over 90,000 visitors in its four weeks in New York, after which it traveled to Chicago and Boston. This was the most significant art exhibition ever shown in the United States. The ideas of Modernism, which up to this point had been confined to Stieglitz's circle at 291 and a small group of collectors, were suddenly unveiled to everyone and American art could no longer continue its complacent path.

Although American artists had always traveled and studied in Europe there had been a time lag between European developments and their American adaptation. Now, for the their first time, European ideas were on display, including the latest movements and the most radical artists.

Two-Dimensionality

The essential characteristic of Modernism was a move away from realistic representation of the world towards a concern with the actual two-dimensionality of the picture surface. Shapes, colors, line, mass, tone, rhythm, and texture all became formal elements in the process of picture-making without resorting to three-dimensional illusion. American artists who had developed their ideas under European Modernism and who had studied with Matisse in 1908 included Max Weber, Alfred Maurer, Arthur G. Dove, Arthur B. Carlos and Patrick Henry Bruce; Marsden Hartley and John Marin also studied in Europe at this time. Although some of these artists had shown in 291, the Armory Show quickened the process of spreading these ideas and opened up public awareness of them.

Arthur G. Dove (1880–1946) spent two years in Paris from 1907 to 1909; in 1912 he painted what is possibly the first American abstract picture, in which forms are selected and organized to express the dynamic qualities that he found in the original motif. He continued this approach into the 1930s and 1940s and it is exemplified by *City Moon* (1938). Dove's work is very close to Kandinsky's of 1910 to 1914 with its echoes of landscape and natural forms. This interest in organic abstraction was shared in the post Armory Show period by Georgia O'Keeffe (see pp. 120–4) but, of all the artists who studied in Paris in the early years of the twentieth century, only Dove seems to have originated his own abstract style before the Armory Show.

John Marin (1870–1953), who studied in Paris from 1905 to 1911, created a personal style based on Cubism. Many of his works are in watercolor, which gives them an immediacy and fluidity – the result of his direct recording of an image. The buildings and lights of Manhattan and the coast of Maine form the basic motifs for these studies. In *Broadway Night* (1929) he uses the geometric shapes of billboards and buildings to capture the dynamism of life in the city. Marin came under the influence of Stieglitz in 1911 when he saw Cézanne's watercolors and the early Cubist work of Picasso at 291. This transformed his work from the early etchings he produced in Paris to a concern with abstract organizations which he developed in his series of New York city paintings. These

John Marin
Broadway Night 1929
21⅜″ × 26⅝″
The Metropolitan Museum
of Art

*J*ohn Marin's distinctive style was originally inspired by
Cubism, which, although tagged as 'abstract', really only dealt
in abstraction from the observed object – be it still life, portrait,
figure group or landscape. Where the originators of the style,
Picasso and Braque, incorporated 'found' objects such as scraps of
newspaper and merchandise labels into their compositions as a
means of tacking the paintings onto a context of reality, Marin
found a similar ready-made imagery in the proliferation of
advertising billboards and illuminated signs in the city center.

    Here he used the device to stabilize the cacophony of movement –
the crowds and traffic – which occupy the foreground of the
painting. Using bright primary colors and leaping contrasts Marin
successfully captures the impact on the senses of Broadway at night.
Marin is also noted for his gentler seascapes, where simple forms
float on delicate washes of blues and greens □

*T*he assimilation and extension of some European ideas (rather than the imitation of them) continued to form an element in American art. But much of this arose from the increasing number of Europeans coming to settle in America. Over 13 million immigrants arrived between 1900 and 1920, and in the inter-war years a stream of exiled Russians, Germans and Jews sought refuge here. Thus a rich mix of alien ideas were absorbed into mainstream American culture.

Max Weber was Russian-born, but had emigrated at the age of ten. Nevertheless his work is characteristic of the blending of a European temperament with the vigor of American idealism. Here he has taken some of the superficial elements of Cubism – the broken, multifaceted image, flat, patterned 'found' surfaces, and organized them to create a hybrid impression of a restaurant at night – the bright surface decorations of the floors, tables and walls and the decorative borders of the architecture framing and enveloping the fragmentary glimpses of the diners themselves. The division between the two elements is much more pronounced than in the more self-consciously harmonious compositions of the European Cubists □

Max Weber
Chinese Restaurant 1915
40″ × 48″
Whitney Museum of
American Art, New York

influences, allied with the changing skyline of the city, generated a chain of spontaneous lyrical paintings from him. In his later works he came closer to abstract expressionism in his effort to show paint as paint, yet until his death in 1953 Marin constantly turned to landscape as the source of his imagery.

Cubism

The assimilation of Cubism was seen in the work of one of the other Americans who had studied under Matisse. Like Marin, the Russian-born painter Max Weber (1881–1961) was taken into the circle of Stieglitz and he even lived for a time at 291, helping to hang exhibitions. His early painting after his return from Paris shows a strong influence of Matisse in the use of flat areas of color but gradually the influence of Picasso and Cubism took over and this is seen in an extreme form in *Chinese Restaurant* (1915) with its complete

*T*he struggle by American artists to free themselves of European influences can be overstated, as can parallels between near contemporary painters on the two continents. The work of Cézanne, of the Cubists and of the Italian Futurists can be cited as playing an influential role on a landscape such as this, but the final effect is far removed from any of those European models.

What is clear from this painting is the emergence of a kind of mathematical or geometric scheme being imposed on the landscape, breaking it down into formal compositional blocks each retaining its own discrete value, while contributing to the harmonious interaction of the whole. The use of non-naturalistic primary colors also contributes to the viewer's recognition that the landscape is merely a springboard for an elaborate orchestration of color and form which succeeds on its own terms as a composition, without direct reference to nature. In achieving this situation, the painting prefigures the refined abstract city-scapes of Joseph Stella □

assimilation of the aesthetics of the Parisian style. The use of a richly textured surface and repeated images combined with fragmented planes ally this painting closely to the analytical Cubism of Picasso and Braque. Picasso's effect on Weber continued in the nudes of the 1920s but by the 1940s it had been replaced by a more expressionist figurative style. Throughout his career Weber absorbed European styles, but his later work does not reach the quality of his early achievements.

Gallery 291 also launched the work of Oscar Bluemner (1867–1938) who, like Weber, showed a strong bias towards Cubism. In his paintings he explored the structure of landscape by exaggerating the cubic forms, displaying echoes of the landscapes of Cézanne. In Bluemner's work, however, the striving of Cézanne to analyze structure has been replaced by a predilection for surface pattern making as in *Morning Light (Dover Hills)* (1912–16).

**Oscar Bluemner
Morning Light (Dover
Hills, October)** c. 1916
20″ × 30⅛″
Hirshhorn Museum and
Sculpture Garden,
Smithsonian Institution

Marsden Hartley
Movement No. 5:
Provincetown Houses 1916
20″ × 16″
The Metropolitan Museum
of Art

Modernism Evolves

Another leading painter in the evolution of Modernism in the United States was Marsden Hartley (1877–1943). His early work of around 1907 displayed Impressionist formats but he added to them a rhythmical surface which produced more than a record of purely visual sensations and the Impressionist color was superseded by a more solid, starker range and handling. Much of his work at this stage was derived from the landscapes of Maine. Expressionist influences, deriving probably from the tradition of Ryder, are apparent in the romantic twisted forms in his painting. Hartley visited Europe in 1912 and absorbed some of the impact of Cubism but his visit to Germany reinforced the expressionist tendencies of his work, producing imagery close to that of Kandinsky. The abstract works with their overtones of war that he produced in Germany had some impact on the art world of Berlin when he exhibited with Der Blaue Reiter (the Blue Rider – the most important modern art group in Germany before 1914) at the invitation of Franz Marc, and on the American art world when he returned in 1916, as American Modernism at this time was dependent on the analytical structural images of Cubism and not these emotionally expressive abstract images. From this point he returned to representational work where images were altered in line with his expressionist tendencies. *Movement Number 5, Provincetown Houses* (1916) comes from this period, and shows a reduction to elemental shapes and simple color dominated by black drawing.

Joseph Stella (1877–1946) was born in Italy and came to the United States at the age of 19 with the intention of entering the medical profession. Like many American artists, Stella entered the art world via magazine illustration and he was one of the group who visited France in 1908 to learn more about the new ideas being generated there. From Paris he went to Italy to study the Futurist movement and it was this combined Cubist/Futurist exposure that manifested itself in his work from the time of the Armory Show onwards. He is especially known for his paintings based on the Brooklyn Bridge which date from this period.

Like Marin, Stella found inspiration in the buildings, lights and bridges of New York. His *View of the City of New York Interpreted* (1920–22) is a five-panel homage to the life of the city and shows the impact of the machine aesthetic which manifested itself in the Futurist movement in the work of artists such as Boccioni and Severini. This image is less fragmented than his earlier Futurist paintings such as *Battle of Light, Coney Island*; the Futurist painters shattered their images into prisms of light and color to demonstrate a sense of movement and Stella's early works after the Armory Show reflect this. In *New York Interpreted* he shows instead the forces inherent in the industrial forms.

In Paris in 1912 and 1913 the ideas of Cubism were extended by Robert Delaunay and Frantisek Kupka into a much looser abstract color structure. Their achievements, known as Orphisme, were paralleled by similar developments in the work of Macdonald-Wright and Morgan Russell, who had been in Paris at this time and who claimed that they had originated these ideas, calling their style Synchromism. It was a style in which color and tone were used in a completely non-figurative way with no reference to anything other than the painting itself. Color itself was 'the generating function'. Stanton Macdonald-Wright (1890–1973) in his painting *Oriental Synchromy in Blue-Green* (1918) exhibits these ideas, which derived from Cézanne's aims of showing form by the optical nature of color – some colors advance, others recede. This style did not last long but it was the most progressive, radical manifestation of abstract art at this time.

The importance of the Armory Show was that it brought a new awareness of the

The monumental qualities of Marsden Hartley's work set him apart from Weber, Bluemner and Stella, as does his primary concentration on the objects of the landscape before him – however simplified and reduced they might be. His interests lay in the interplay between austere, simple and historical architectural forms (the object) and their representation in thickly applied fields of muted color paint (the subject).

The final result is similar, in its tension between the abstract and tactile qualities of the painted surface, and the somber, brooding mood evoked by his images, to Albert Pinkham Ryder's work. The

rough edges and lack of finish in Hartley's work also distance him from his more formally polished and geometrically exact abstract contemporaries, and introduce a note of Expressionism into his work which promotes the psychological impact of his landscape and townscape compositions □

emerging American ideas in art but its drawback, from the artists' viewpoint, was the comparison with their more famous French contemporaries. The established styles of realism and American Impressionism were finally devalued and even the movement which had been considered radical – the Eight, or Ash Can School – was seen as tentative in comparison to the radical ideas imported from Europe. One of the primary intentions of the Armory Show had been to promote American art and in this aim it was not successful; museums were still not interested in buying or showing American Modernist paintings. However, private collectors began to corner this market, and some of the major modern collections were begun at that time.

The social disruption created by the First World War was not echoed in American art and it would have been strange if it had been so. The art produced prior to the war was not aimed at social change so it did not adopt such a policy during it. Even in Europe, where the effects of war were so much more immediate, the only reference to it in art was the nihilistic tendencies which gave birth to the Dada movement, but these tendencies were already evident in the Modernist movement before the war.

**Stanton Macdonald-Wright
'Oriental' Synchromy in
Blue-Green** 1918
36″ × 50″
Whitney Museum of
American Art, New York

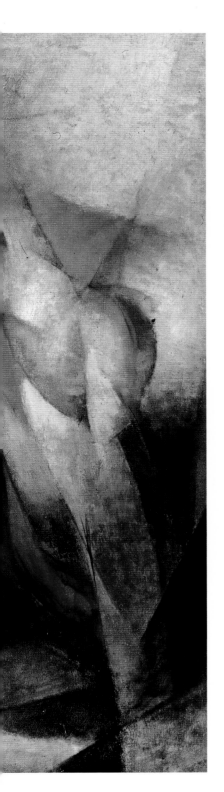

*B*y the end of the second decade of the twentieth century the abstract impulse in American art had successfully moved the American Dream landscape onto a new path. The abstract artists introduced a new positivism and aesthetic freedom which suggested once more a great future for America – after all the land of the free. This attitude was probably fostered by a great upsurge in wealth and opportunity at the time, and by America's embarkation on a policy of confident empire-building. All things seemed possible to the lucky inhabitants of the world's youngest Great Power, and this was reflected in the arts.

Stanton Macdonald-Wright's painting extended the notion of a pure harmonic balance of form and color previously posited by Arthur Dove and Oscar Bluemner to a state approaching perfection. But there remains here tension between the motifs, for at the center of the interlocking and overlapping planes which hint at human forms is a curious blue hemisphere seemingly emanating light – a rising sun maybe – which refers back across the decades to the warm distant glows of the Luminist painters.

Joseph Stella remains the towering genius of the first generation of American urban abstract painters, the visual poet of the American Jazz Age. His paintings freely embrace the dynamism and tectonic power of what was then the foremost modern architectural landscape in the world – New York. Where artists such as Bluemner sought to impose ordered structures upon the landscape, conjuring these up by reducing form and color to neat equations, Stella recognized the beauty of the mechanical structures behind the façades of the modern city – the steel skeletons which made it possible to construct skyscrapers, the graceful cantilevers and suspension cables of overhead railroads and bridges. Stella brought these to the core of his compositions, enriching these harsh forms with primary colors and the glint of polished steel and chrome, scattering the reflective surfaces with the clear strong light of artificial electric illumination. This majestic polyptych is an elegiac hymn to the beauty of technology, not only in its most manifest form – the New York skyline – but in all the intricacies and complexities of the urban infrastructure □

Joseph Stella
The Voice of the City of
New York Interpreted
1920–22
Central panel: 99¾″ × 54″
Outer panels: 88½″ × 54″
Newark Museum

Native Realism

Much art work was produced during the war in the way of propaganda posters to stimulate patriotism but this was not significant and it had no effect on the course of art in America. (A rather bizarre artistic war effort was the production of landscape targets. These were exhibited in the Salmagundi Club and in the Arden Gallery in 1918 and then destroyed as targets for teaching rifle shooting.) After the war the intellectual elite rejected their former idealism and adopted a cynicism in which they saw capitalism without its democratic veneer. However, art continued its isolated existence by producing luxury objects for the wealthy. There was a sense of experimentation as a result of the Armory Show and the adoption of European Modernism but, over the course of the 1920s, many of the Modernist ideas of abstraction were rejected or at least subordinated to native realism.

One far-reaching result of the first World War was the adoption of rigid immigration policies by Congress in 1921, 1924 and 1929, and there was an era of reactionary feeling which found expression in the United States refusing an invitation to send American art to an exhibition in Paris in 1925. Within America, however, there was a growing art awareness, with the opening of over 60 new museums between 1921 and 1930. The golden age of the 'roaring twenties' was a period of immense wealth which lasted until Autumn 1929, when the collapse of the stock market heralded the Great Depression of the thirties. During this dark period many artists received help from the government in the guise of the Federal Art Projects of the Works Progress Administration, which was established in 1935 and provided work for unemployed artists and exposure for their paintings. It was a massive experiment, employing the talents of thousands of painters, sculptors and designers including artists of future renown such as Ben Shahn, Philip Evergood, John Steuart Curry, Grant Wood and Jackson Pollock.

In the 1930s the US government commissioned over 2,000 murals from artists, only a few of which went beyond illustration. The most notable artists involved were Willem de Kooning, Stuart Davis, Arshile Gorky and Thomas Hart Benton. In addition the Works Progress Administration helped other artists by giving them a regular monthly allowance for each art project, and this lasted from 1935–1943. The contribution of this program varied in that much of the work produced was not of a very high standard, but it did allow artists such as Jackson Pollock to experiment by working on their painting full time. It was also important in bringing art to the people in its organized traveling exhibitions.

The 1930s saw an influx of fresh talent from Europe in the form of refugees from the rise of nationalism in Germany and Russia. Many of these were major intellectual and artistic figures in Western culture – people such as Walter Gropius, Mies van der Rohe, George Gross, Lyonel Feininger, Thomas Mann, Bertolt Brecht, Erwin Panofsky and Albert Einstein. The impact on American culture and on the art world was far-reaching; many of the artist refugees accepted influential teaching posts and their ideas were thereby propagated in the future generations. The result of these political upheavals was that the period of the 1920s and 1930s was one of immense richness and diversity of ideas in art.

The Precisionists

The combination of native realism with the Cubist approach of European Modernism can be seen in the work of Charles Sheeler and Charles Demuth. Charles Sheeler (1883–1965) was the most consistent of the group known as the Precisionists, whose work is characterized by precise detail and clearly structured images. Many of his paintings such as *River Rouge Plant* (1932) were produced at the Ford plants and echo the preoccupation of many artists with the machine age. In this work we see a total rejection of the nineteenth-century artists' concern with nature and in its place is substituted a landscape created by man with stark geometric patterns predominating. Unlike Joseph Stella, who derived his imagery from similar sources, Sheeler did not fragment or distort his subject to capture the dynamism of the machine age but painted it in a precise, clearly defined way – a classical kind of landscape in which all is clear and still. In its control and order it resembles some of the work of Winslow Homer. Sheeler's earlier work after the Armory Show relied heavily on Cubism, but he abandoned this in 1920 in the search for realism simplified by Cubist references. One of the major influences in the production of this

Charles Sheeler
River Rouge Plant 1932
20″ × 24″
Whitney Museum of
American Art, New York

*D*espite the considerable sophistication of American abstract painting by the 1920s, there remained a strong vein of naturalistic representation which embraced the modern American landscape. The industrial capacity of American industry expanded greatly in the first 30 years of the twentieth century – not only in the traditional centers of the North East, but in the Mid West as well.

Sheeler was influenced early in his career by Cubism and by Synchromism, but soon found that the real forms of industrial technology and architecture, rendered in a Precisionist style resembling engineer's drawings, provided him with sufficient 'natural' motifs to create resonant, even monumental, images of the contemporary American landscape. In the century or so which divided Sheeler from the Hudson River painters, the American landscape had, for most people, been transformed from one of immense natural beauty to one reflecting the face of human endeavor and exploitation □

painting was the camera; Sheeler was involved in clear focus photography from 1917 through the 1920s.

The work of Charles Demuth (1883–1935) is much more varied than that of Sheeler. His early work, around 1915, was of free watercolor landscapes but under the guidance of Stieglitz he began to experiment with a more formal structure of abstract rhythms which then led to a type of abstraction based on Cubism in which directional lines and planes were created – a combination of Cubism and Futurism. Around 1920, Demuth started working in tempera and then in oil on industrial landscapes. Even with these media he suppressed any painterly qualities and used them in a crisp way as in *My Egypt* (1927). The influence of Marcel Duchamp is also apparent in some of his work in the use of letters

Charles Demuth
My Egypt 1927
35¾″ × 30″
Whitney Museum of
American Art, New York

*C*harles Demuth straddled the twin areas occupied by the abstract modernist Joseph Stella and the Precisionist Charles Sheeler. Like Sheeler, he often concentrated on the industrial landscape, stripped of its messy accretions and seen rather as a clean, bright image of modernism. The overall image is built up to give a sharp decorative effect dominated primarily by the delicate interaction of shape and color within an essentially hard-edged compositional format. If Stella's work provides a counterpart to the music of the age, then Demuth's paintings sit easily alongside the literary imagery of William Carlos Williams and John Dos Passos.

A number of influential European artists arrived in the United States as a result of the Nazi Party takeover in Germany. Born to German parents in America, Lyonel Feininger worked in Europe,

returning to the USA in 1936. In France he had been associated with the development of geometric Cubism (Section d'Or), and in Germany with the Blaue Reiter group and had taught at the Bauhaus.

Architectural motifs were the most compatible subjects for his style – and we can see here how Cubism operated in direct contrast to a style such as Impressionism; where the latter tended to suppress the physical actuality of solid tangible objects into a suffused glow of light and color, here light and color are combined with the same physical presence as the solid masonry of the buildings □

**Lyonel Charles Adrian
Feininger
The Church at Gelmeroda**
1936, 39½″ × 31⅝″
The Metropolitan Museum
of Art

and numbers such as in *I Saw The Figure Five In Gold* (1928), a homage to the poet William Carlos Williams.

The denial of the sensuous element of pigment is evident in Demuth's painting and is characteristic of much American realism. In his oil painting of *My Egypt* there is a detachment and clinicalism that also appears in the work of Homer, Sheeler and Wyeth, but there is a delicacy of color in much of his work which is not apparent in most of the other Modernist painters and Demuth stands as one of the innovators of the early twentieth century.

The Cubist/Futurist vocabulary with its directional lines and flattened geometric shapes that appears in Demuth's painting is also seen in the work of Lyonel Feininger (1871–1956) who, though born in the United States, was associated with Der Blaue Reiter group and the Bauhaus in Germany, where he grew up and worked until 1936 when he returned to the United States. Although he spent the majority of his life outside America his work is close to Demuth's and the Precisionists' as can be seen in his painting *Gelmeroda. Number 13* (1936). The resemblance is superficial, for Feininger's painting is not so clinical as Demuth's and it exploits the actual surface in a painterly fashion unlike the detachment of Demuth. This painterly involvement is probably the result of Feininger's European training.

Georgia O'Keeffe (1887–1986) painted in a similarly precise style, but rejected the man-made landscapes that attracted Sheeler and Demuth for natural forms. From the time of the Armory Show O'Keeffe worked in an abstract style based on natural forms which derived from close-ups of plants and flowers. She became a member of Stieglitz's circle when, in 1916, he exhibited in Gallery 291 some of her abstract drawings which had been shown to him by a friend of hers without her knowledge. The following year she had a one-man show at his gallery – the first of many – and in 1924 they were married.

Her work ranges from the freely painted canvases such as *Portrait W. No 11, 1917* to the hard-edged Precisionist close-ups of the 1920s for which she is best known. Once she had established this precise style of painting she retained it throughout her life. Although her paintings alternate between the close-up figurative pictures of plants and her abstract

Georgia O'Keeffe
Red Hills and the Sun,
Lake George 1927
27″ × 32″
The Phillips Collection,
Washington DC

Georgia O'Keeffe
Black Place II 1944
23⅞″ × 30″
The Metropolitan Museum
of Art

Georgia O'Keeffe was one of the towering figures of twentieth-century American art, not merely because of the proliferation and consistency of her painting, but due to her continued development through nearly all the major phases of American abstract painting, from its first inception between 1910 and 1920. She was also one of the few painters whose relationship with the American landscape ranged from the cityscapes of New York to the desolation of the South-West, where eventually she settled.

Surprisingly, her painting remained fundamentally unified in its careful interplay between hard-edged and natural forms, between accentuated lights and darks, between external observation and interior psychological reaction.

At the core of her work is the paradoxical tension between the desolation of the American landscape, at its darkest and most awe-inspiring, and the delicate natural beauty which lives within that landscape. It is a theme which has largely supplanted the Romantic vision of the nineteenth century in the modern American mythology □

*T*he limited structural framework and bright expressive
notations of Black American popular music – jazz and blues –
provided Stuart Davis with a direct source of inspiration for his
deceptively simple large-scale compositions. His forms were derived
from a reduction of Cubist technique to pure outline, such depth as
exists arising from the juxtaposition of strongly contrasting colors.
Into these complex interactions Davis often introduced more
familiar imagery – signwriting, the moon and stars, city skylines –
in order to tack the composition onto a framework of collective visual
experience.

This mixture of style and imagery manages to avoid being
'difficult' and appeals directly to popular sensitivities in much the
same way as jazz music – a combination of the expressive and
colorful set within a familiar and accessible format □

Stuart Davis
Study for Swing Landscape
1938
22″ × 28¾″
The Corcoran Gallery of Art

works they are in no way contradictory but are in effect concerned with the same ideas of composition, no matter what the subject or its treatment.

Much of her working life was spent in the desertlands of New Mexico; in 1945 she bought a house there and after the death of Stieglitz settled there for the rest of her life, using the desert and the bleached animal bones and skulls that she found in it as inspiration for many of her paintings. Her landscapes such as *Black Place II* (1944) echo the starkness and the color of the New Mexican country, but retain a strong link with the rest of her painting in their selectiveness and precision of handling. The continuing popularity of Georgia O'Keeffe's work is because its hints at figuration and its 'polished' surface make the abstractions of Modernism understandable to many.

The Jazz Age

The 1920s in America was also known as the Jazz Age and the music of jazz, the skyline of American cities and the speed of the automobile all find expression in the paintings of Stuart Davis (1894–1964). Davis' father was the art editor of the *Philadelphia Press* when the Ash Can artists Glackens, Shinn, Luks, Sloan and Henri were employed as illustrators. Stuart Davis was trained by Robert Henri for three years and exhibited some watercolors in the style of the Ash Can School in the Armory Show. From this point onwards Davis fell under the spell of the avant-garde European painting, specifically Cubism and the color of the Fauves.

In the 1920s he evolved his own style of precise shapes with glowing colors assembled on the canvas to counteract any suggestion of three-dimensional space. The images are much harsher and brasher than those of Sheeler, Demuth and O'Keeffe and they attempt to capture the dynamic atmosphere of the city. It is a style based on Synthetic Cubism, the successor in Paris to Analytical Cubism, in which the planes of the latter are reassembled and combined with letters and numbers. The 'rawness' of the imagery is apparent in *Study for Swing Landscape* (1938) which has in the flatness of the painted surface some of the character of a Matisse collage. Davis has always acknowledged his debt, and the debt of American artists generally, to Europe but has also insisted that the impulse for the creation of his work is the American landscape – the skyscrapers, the city, movies and jazz.

The life of New York city, especially the seamier side of it, was the inspiration of another artist who captures the atmosphere of the Great Depression – Reginald Marsh (1898–1954). This was also the era of the reawakening of figurative art from the shadow of Modernism which had dominated art for two decades. For the figurative artists of the 1930s the subject was, as in Marsh's painting, the American scene – a continuation of the themes of the Ash Can School at the turn of the century. However, their work differed from the Ash Can School in its more sophisticated technique and coloring which was adopted from the lessons of the Modernists.

Like the Ash Can painters, Marsh had worked as an illustrator for various publications including *Vanity Fair* and *Harper's Bazaar*. His subjects ranged from the down-and-outs of *The Bowery* (1930) through the densely populated beaches at Rockaway and Coney Island, and the life of New York nightclubs. Many of his paintings reflected the life of the unemployed and the homeless, the lines at unemployment exchanges and the derelicts on park benches. This was a dark period in American history when one third of the working population was unemployed and Marsh captured the spirit of the age in his canvases.

The revival of figurative art and the impetus given to public works by the Federal Art Projects of the Works Progress Administration program, plus the obsession with the social problems of the age, triggered a renewed search for an American style. This nationalism in art also produced a chauvinism which denied the debt owed to European art and especially to the concepts generated by the Modernist movement. It materialized in a provincial movement of Regionalism, of which John Steuart Curry (1897–1946) was one of the leading landscape artists. Curry, too, worked as a magazine illustrator, moving on to painting in the 1930s. From 1936 to his death in 1946 he taught art at the University of Wisconsin, where he promoted his ideas of Regionalism and his rejection of European sources. His *Wisconsin Landscape* (1938–39) dates from his early years at the University and is typical of his subject matter in the depiction of the stormy sky over the large-scale

Reginald Marsh
The Bowery 1930
48″ × 36″
The Metropolitan Museum
of Art

*T*he crash of the US dollar in 1929 and the ensuing worldwide economic depression drew many artists back to the social problems first examined by Henri and the Ash Can School in the early years of the century. Many of the workers who had crowded into the industrial cities in the boom years now found themselves out of work and dependent upon welfare and soup kitchens for daily survival.

Reginald Marsh turned his attention to the derelicts on the very bottom rung of the collapsing social ladder, and gave back to them a sense of robust energy and dignity which, in microcosm, reflected a more general search among American artists for a fundamental cultural identity in the wake of the trauma of the Wall Street Crash □

landscape. Violence or the suggestion of it is often visible in his work, either of the elements as in *Tornado over Kansas* or of animals as in *Hogs killing Rattlesnakes*. Although Curry went to Paris for one year and also studied in New York and Chicago he returned to the Mid West which he continued to use as the inspiration for his painting.

Thomas Hart Benton (1889–1975) was another champion of Regionalism and the Mid West. Like Curry, Benton studied in both Paris and Chicago and like Curry he returned to middle America. Although claiming to reject Modernism Benton's work owes something to the movement in its use of exaggeration and unrealistic color, while in the distortion of his figures in his late paintings he shows the influence of sixteenth-century Mannerism.

The characteristics evident in *July Hay* (1943) of a flattened space and exaggerated postures of the figures are partly the result of his method of working from clay models.

John Steuart Curry
Wisconsin Landscape
1938–39
42″ × 84″
The Metropolitan Museum
of Art

*I*n reaction to the work of the abstract painters a number of more down-to-earth realists began to emerge in the years following the Great War. Foremost among these was Edward Hopper. Hopper's work was unusual in combining in equal parts urban and rural scenes, for many of this new wave of Realists consciously emphasized their particular, largely non-urban, backgrounds and roots, and they came to be known as the Regionalists. At a time when country blues and folk music were beginning to define a popular identity for the workers, the oppressed and the blacks, so the Regionalist painters began to define in paint that vast agglomeration of local views and values which could only now be recognized as the true historical landscape of America.

Regionalism attempted to look beyond the American fondness for yarn-spinning and myth-making at the real historical and cultural values of America at large. It is notable too that novelists such as Thornton Wilder and Sherwood Anderson were exploring the same vein. Unfortunately, the myths often got in the way, and a painter such as Thomas Hart Benton eventually did more to further than to dispel them. However some, such as John Steuart Curry seen here, did manage to turn a fresh, uncluttered eye on the American landscape of the time, to telling and charming effect □

The ruralism and social realism of his approach are seen in his mural series which were painted for the new School for Social Research in 1930 and the Whitney Museum of American Art in 1932; these murals show the richness of American life from agriculture to industrialization and, in the criticism they contain of city life, they demonstrate his sympathy for the rural scene.

The Muralists

The social comments on American life seen in the Regionalists' work was much fiercer in the art of the Mexican muralists Orozco, Siqueiros and Rivera, and it was with Rivera that Ben Shahn (1898–1969), an immigrant Lithuanian, worked on the Rockefeller Center murals. Shahn's work, with its realist style, has a strong vein of social comment running through it and his series of 23 paintings of the trial and execution of the radical agitators Sacco and Vanzetti, painted in 1931 and 1932, brought him notoriety as a protest painter. Not all of his paintings have such strong political leanings, however. Many are about city life, an extension of the ideas of the Ash Can School, but Shahn has absorbed the contribution of the Modernists in the abstract design of his compositions. In *Handball* (1939) the pattern of the figures against the blank wall shows a link with the Precisionists in its design and in the incorporation of lettering.

Regionalism as a movement was shortlived. The influx of European artists in the thirties fleeing the terrors of their own countries and the participation of the United States in World War II after the bombing of Pearl Harbor by the Japanese brought to an end America's brief artistic isolation and heralded a renewed global involvement in all aspects of society.

The Realist Tradition Continues

The establishment of the Society of Abstract Artists in New York in 1936, while promoting the concepts of non-figurative painting and sounding the death knell for Regionalism and chauvinism, did not destroy the realist tradition and the two most famous realist American painters of the twentieth century are Edward Hopper and Andrew Wyeth.

Edward Hopper (1882–1967) trained under Robert Henri and then Kenneth Hayes Miller (who also trained Reginald Marsh and many of the urban realists of the 1930s). Visits to France also affected Hopper's painting in the awareness and understanding of light – a major element in all his work. The Armory Show sold one of his paintings but it was in 1933, when the Museum of Modern Art in New York gave him a large exhibition, that he suddenly gained fame. Perhaps it is in Hopper that the search for an American tradition finds fulfilment. His is an art about landscape – American landscape – and even when his paintings include people they are often isolated and trapped within a frozen environment. However, his canvases are more often of places; buildings at a certain time of day under a certain condition of light, such as his *Early Sunday Morning* (1930), an uncompromising, straightforward painting of a row of stores in the same Luminist tradition that reappeared in the Precisionists. Hopper spoke of rejecting French domination of American art but the influence of the French and European traditions is important in the development of Hopper's work, though it is composed not of a mere

Thomas Hart Benton
July Hay 1943
38″ × 26¾″
The Metropolitan Museum of Art

*T*he impact of the Great Depression rapidly spread beyond the obvious pressure points of the larger industrial centers, and permeated even the usually stable rural agricultural areas. The economic crisis here was made worse by the baleful fruits of unwise long-term cropping policies, which now brought infertility and crop-failure, and which laid millions of acres open to devastation by flood or drought, as in the famous Kansas 'dust-bowl'. Rural families were brought to the brink of starvation and ruin. Traditional American faith in the beneficence of the land was fundamentally undermined.

President Roosevelt's New Deal policies, inaugurated in the 1930s, were largely devoted to a restructuring of the economic landscape of the United States, and one aspect of this regeneration was the establishment of the Federal Art Project (WPA) which was designed to restore a sense of unity and faith in a common national culture based on fundamental truths.

Thomas Hart Benton was only one of a number of painters who, working within the tenets of the WPA guidelines, did much to remind Americans of their very real cultural heritage and the nobility of the basic values of family life, hard work and Christian morality □

A movement such as the WPA could never escape the arena of
political comment, especially during the period between 1929
and America's entry into the Second World War in December 1941.
Social unrest was rife throughout the US during this period with
waves of strikes and factory sit-downs, the development of extremist
factions on both the Right and the Left, and racial hatred spreading
from its traditional spawning ground south of the Mason-Dixon
line to the burgeoning and increasingly mixed-race cities of the
northern States of America.

The rural Regionalists often managed to skirt these issues, but
even among them, in the work of painters such as Charles
Burchfield, the specter of an uncertain future nevertheless seems to
haunt their landscapes.

Among the urban Realists few were as successful as Ben Shahn
at articulating, with quiet, rational understatement, their awareness
of the appalling social and political problems facing America. His
cityscapes were peopled by street characters who seem stoically to
accept their lot, and indeed get on with the daily business of
humdrum survival. His work looks forward to the great wave of
social awareness in the arts – especially in literature and the cinema
– which immediately followed the war, and which came to a boiling
point in the Communist witch-hunts of the late 1940s □

Ben Shahn
Handball 1939
Tempera on paper over composition board 22¾″ × 31¼″
The Museum of Modern Art, New York, Abby Aldrich Rockefeller Fund

Edward Hopper
Early Sunday Morning
1930
35″ × 60″
Whitney Museum of
American Art, New York

acceptance of ideas but of an adaptation and incorporation into his own personal vision; there are echoes of the art of Degas, who used space and figures to create compositional tensions in a similar way to Hopper, while the influence of Modernism is apparent in the underlying formal structure of *Early Sunday Morning* and in many of his other paintings. We see the same concerns in *Rooms by the Sea* (1951) where broad masses of light and shadow create his world of timelessness. The whole picture is handled with a painterly quality which gives life to the simple shapes.

The subjects of isolation and loneliness which dominated Hopper's work were also important themes in the paintings of his contemporary, Andrew Wyeth (b. 1917). Unlike the painterly style of Hopper, however, Wyeth takes a photographic style of rendering everything in meticulous detail. It is a style which has great popular appeal in its evident

*E*dward Hopper's method of approaching the social and political problems of American society between the wars was no less telling than that employed by Shahn, but was considerably more poetic and dealt almost exclusively with landscape. He was capable of extracting from an ordinary city street or small-town sidewalk an immensely poignant and unsettling aura of desolation and loneliness, as if the rich social fabric which had produced these arcades had suddenly been erased, leaving the shells of houses, with faceless windows, as mute archaeological artifacts.

When people do appear in Hopper's work, they are ciphers, isolated, hunched figures for whom communication with their fellow kind is a forgotten art. The atmosphere of his paintings, like those of Shahn, look forward to the desolate hard lights and deep shadows of films noirs *and of the existentialist hard-boiled novels of Jim Thompson and James M. Cain* □

degree of skill and continues the tradition of artists such as Mount and Eakins. Wyeth used tempera for paintings and built up his images in small, delicate strokes of paint. His best-known work is probably *Christina's World* (1948), in which every blade of grass is rendered with the same precision as the detail of the crippled figure of Christina and the house on the hill. The overall effect resembles a tonal drawing in its very limited color range.

The strongest influence on Wyeth was probably that of his father, who was a famous illustrator of stories by Robert Louis Stephenson and James Fenimore Cooper. Andrew

The poetic intensity which Hopper was capable of conjuring up, when blended with his strange sense of isolation, could often place his work on the borders of Surrealism. Sometimes, as here, he accentuated these qualities the better to achieve a genuinely disturbing effect. In this his painting is comparable to the dream landscapes of the Italian Giorgio de Chirico or the Belgian René Magritte; with the latter Hopper shared a peculiar ability to render everyday objects in paint in a manner which was superficially 'realistic' and yet which at the same time seemed to deny their representational solidity, placing them firmly and irretrievably in the painted realm, just beyond the viewer's grasp.

In later life Hopper concentrated increasingly on landscapes and seascapes in New England, and the sea began to take on the role given the city in his early work – a symbolic force representing the isolation of mankind from his surroundings □

Wyeth was ill as a child and consequently was educated at home, where he was exposed to an environment rich in art. Under his father's tutelage he learned the draftsmanship which continued as the strongest element in his work. In Wyeth's painting the emphasis on the particular occasionally detracts from the overall tonal unity; *Christina's World* is an exception to this and is one of his most successful works.

The simplified figurative tradition established in Stieglitz's artists under the impact of European Modernism continued through the thirties and beyond into the post-World War II period with the work of Milton Avery (1885–1965), as can be seen in his

Edward Hopper
Rooms by the Sea 1951
29″ × 40⅛″
Yale University Art Gallery

The work of America's leading Realist painter, Andrew Wyeth, stands both comparison and contrast with that of Hopper. Wyeth established early in his career a dense personal mythology in which a continuing narrative can be perceived – he has rarely strayed in his painting from his native Maine, and his cast of characters is drawn from his neighbors. One of them, the paralyzed Christina, was a recurring character. These people are portrayed with an

objective compassion which invites us to become involved with the artist's own problems in perceiving and communicating with his subjects. This can lead to mawkishness and this painting – one of the great icons of modern American art – undoubtedly draws simultaneously on sentimentality and gothic chill. But it is Wyeth's peculiar approach to landscape which finally captures the onlooker's attention. Working usually in tempera – a difficult medium – Wyeth

Andrew Wyeth
Christina's World 1948
Tempera on gesso panel
32¼″ × 47¾″
The Museum of Modern Art,
New York. Purchase

*makes clear the technical problems he has had in fixing, with
magical intensity, the look and feel of the surface of the landscape –
grass, pebbles, leaves, twigs – onto his canvas. In
wandering away from recognizable figures and objects, the viewer
might be forgiven for mistaking areas of Wyeth's canvases for the
work of an abstract expressionist such as Mark Tobey or Jackson
Pollock* □

landscape painting *Spring Orchard* (1959). In this painting Avery owes a debt to the simplified drawing and shapes of Matisse, though they are treated in a more painterly manner. Avery used his landscape as a vehicle for emphasizing color relationships and had no interest in specific places or moments as had Hopper and Wyeth.

Never departing completely from figurative art, Avery stands in that transitional stage between realism and abstraction searching for the essentials of a situation rather than its appearance. His approach to his work was to record direct from landscape in notebooks, his notes translating in his studio into watercolors and oil paintings. Each process was a

way of stripping away the detail to arrive at the essentials, which consisted of areas of color often bounded by a simplified outline.

The Influence of Abstract Expressionism

The compromise between realism and abstraction which persisted in the work of Milton Avery was exploited in the 1950s by Larry Rivers (b. 1923). Music was an important force in the evolution of his work, and art did not come to the forefront of his life until the 1940s after he had worked as a jazz musician for several years. In the 1940s he enrolled in

*T*he figurative tradition as established by the Regionalists and Realists of the 1920s and 1930s has remained a central strand in American art ever since. Milton Avery remained true to the figurative tradition, producing landscapes, often with figures, which combined clearly identifiable form with the textures, nuances and grand manner of the color field painters and the hard-edge painters of the 1950s. Here the delicate balance between controlled drawing in paint, the invited accident consequent upon the flow of paint across the canvas and the blotching effect achieved as the paint dries has created a wonderfully balanced and restrained image strongly reminiscent of some Japanese watercolor painting.

The eclectic work of the prodigiously talented painter, sculptor, designer and graphic artist Larry Rivers has led him to be associated with a number of movements from Abstract Expressionism to Pop Art. However, the root of his work is similar to that of Avery in its adherence to the figurative tradition while experimenting with a broad range of painterly solutions to the pictorial problem. Unlike Avery, Rivers is principally an observer, an artist who draws on his immediate surroundings, albeit enjoying a wide range of reference. His central concern remains the traditional predicament of the painter – what to select from the material available, and how best to render that selection in terms of composition, color and brushwork □

Milton Avery
Spring Orchard 1959
50″ × 66¼″
National Museum of
American Art, Smithsonian
Institution

Larry Rivers
July 1956
83¼″ × 90¼″
The Brooklyn Museum

the school of Hans Hoffman, where he spent two years exploring and developing his ability; he was also influenced by an exhibition of the paintings of the French Intimist painter Pierre Bonnard, and this can be seen in many of his interior paintings of figures and still life objects such as *The Sitter* (1956). Recognition came early, with shows in the fifties, during which time he also visited Paris and Italy. His name was often linked with the Abstract Expressionists, but he has always retained a strong figurative element in his work and the literary connotations are often very important. Several of his paintings refer to earlier works such as Leutze's *Washington Crossing the Delaware*, Eakins' *Rowers*, Rembrandt's *Polish Rider* and Jacques Louis David's *Napoleon Bonaparte in His Study*, but they are adapted or combined in Rivers' painting to produce a completely new image with literary, as well as visual, meaning. For example, his adaptation of David's *Napoleon Bonaparte in His Study* resulted in a multiple image of Napoleon entitled *The Greatest Homosexual* (1964).

His work combines the spontaneity of the Abstract Expressionists with a strong linear structure in which certain figurative elements are emphasized while other parts of the picture are merely suggested or even left empty. This style, which developed in the 1950s while he was staying at Southampton, has continued in varying forms throughout his career. The logical spatial structure of most figurative works in which objects are depicted on a horizontal ground plane is discarded in later Rivers paintings and scale and space are adjusted to conform to his personal vision. This way of combining images is something that appears in the 1960s in the work of the Pop Artists but Rivers maintains a painterly handling with glazes of color and rhythmic charcoal drawing.

July (1956) is a landscape painting from Rivers' Southampton period in which the logical spatial structure is still retained but there is also the seminal form of his mature style in his selective accenting of fragments of objects – a part of a face, a suggestion of a tree, a shorthand notation for the pattern on a shirt. All these contribute to the rhythmical musical quality of his work.

Pop Art

The combining of disparate figurative elements in a non-logical spatial setting which occurs in much of Larry Rivers' mature work is also seen in the paintings of his contemporary Robert Rauschenberg (b. 1925), one of the leading American exponents of Pop Art in the early 1960s. Most of the images used in his work are taken from photographs in newspapers or magazines and combined with letters and numbers, all handled in a painterly style closely related to the art of the Abstract Expressionists. Much Pop Art of the sixties tried to remove the mark of the artist from the painting by the use of a flat, unbroken surface or by reproduction via mechanical means such as the screen printing process as in Andy Warhol's *Soup Cans* or Roy Lichtenstein's enlargements of comic strip imagery. Rauschenberg, however, retained and even emphasized the artist's involvement by his use of gestural brushwork as in *Canyon* (1959).

The Pop Artists of the United States saw in their own consumer society, with its disposable lifestyle, material which would form the subjects of their paintings. For Rauschenberg the material became the actual disposed material – the junk of society – which he collaged on to his canvases to construct his images. His paintings became three-dimensional objects combining painted imagery, collaged textures and attached objects such as the stuffed eagle and pillow on *Canyon*. The Modernists' rejection of illusionist

Robert Rauschenberg
Reservoir 1961
85½″ × 62½″ × 14¾″
National Museum of American Art, Smithsonian Institution

*R*obert Rauschenberg, with Jasper Johns, was foremost among the American avant-garde painters of the 1950s and 1960s, whose association with Pop Art belied their strong appreciation of stylistic and iconographic traditions. Rauschenberg especially draws on the viewer's notions of these traditions, and encourages the viewer to contextualize his compositions, most usually by giving his works definite and provocative titles.

Many of Rauschenberg's painting/collages in the late 1950s and 1960s were given specific landscape titles, inviting the onlooker to participate in a notional reconstruction of such a landscape from the materials the artist has assembled. Thus it is arguable that here we are given a horizon line and blue tones suggesting water; but at what point our interpretation of the piece as a 'landscape' ceases and our involvement with the found and ready-made objects assembled within the painterly suggestion of landscape begins becomes part of the object of the piece □

*T*he question of how we perceive visual experience – landscapes, townscapes, other people – was the central concern of the Super Realists. At its most obvious level Super Realism dealt with the fascination of creating a facsimile which gives the closest possible illusion of reality. Estes however has concentrated on two strands of visual perception initially suggested by photography: the strange flattening of space and deep focus created by the photographic plate; and the 'accuracy' of the photographic image, which goes beyond visual experience to create an artificial, single-focus image which bears little relation to the way we actually see.

Estes sees photography merely as 'a sketch to be used'. The result confounds the viewer not only in its veracity to photographic experience, but in its denial of the validity of mere photography as an acceptable means of representing visual experience. Estes' work has concentrated on city streets and vitrine-glass shop fronts, and in this represents a straightforward record of the late twentieth-century American city □

Richard Estes
Ansonia 1977
48″ × 60″
Whitney Museum of
American Art, New York

space in the painting was taken a step further by impinging on the space of the spectator. It was a challenge by the artist to the aesthetics of traditional art and the hierarchy of 'fine' art versus the untransformed object. This challenge was made more blatant by the use of refuse material.

The introduction of ready-made artifacts into the art world, presented as art objects, was not a new phenomenon. Marcel Duchamp had already exhibited a urinal entitled *Fountain* in New York in 1917 – one of a series of existing objects which he designated as art and which became known as 'ready-mades'. However Rauschenberg combines them with a painted surface which is as sensuous and painterly as in any previous art movement. *Reservoir* (1961) shows the connection of his work to the Abstract Expressionists such as Willem de Kooning in its handling of the actual surface of the canvas while he successfully integrates such foreign objects as clocks, a spoked wheel, an old red board, sacking, and tin cans. The integration is achieved by the use of paint to echo some of the objects' colors or to complement them by figurative association – for example the blue and pink suggestion of sky and the earth colors and cans representing the banks of the reservoir. The objects might be apparently random but the unification of all these elements is very carefully structured.

These works by Rauschenberg still have connections with the traditional aesthetic of the art object – the painting, or the sculpture, as a unique physical element – and not all his work falls into this category. Much of his energies have been devoted to transient works such as performances which opened the boundaries of art to theater and dance, much as the Dadaists had attempted in the early part of the century with their Cabaret Voltaire in 1916 in Zurich.

The impact of Pop art on the American art world was considerable and offered an alternative to the Abstract Expressionists while reinforcing the predilection in the United States for realism or realist elements in art. It provided a link with the traditional imagery of previous movements while utilizing new material and expressing new ideas.

Super Realism

The tradition of realism in art continued in a group of artists who looked to photographic sources for their images. The camera has had an impact on art forms ever since its invention – firstly as an aid to recording information, a kind of visual notebook, then as a means of creating a new approach to composition as seen in Degas and the Impressionists. In the 1970s it was used in New Realism or Super Realism – an art of extreme illusion. Like Pop Artists, the Super Realists took as their subjects everyday situations and like the Impressionists they aimed at a kind of non-composition, an attempt to record exactly what was seen without any kind of transforming of objects. The contemporary environment was their subject and existing images such as photographs,

Strong gestural marks build up the surface of this canvas. There is a progression from the underlying thin stains of color to the later impasto strokes. The intuitive structuring of the painting by the interplay of tonal and color variations achieves a balance between pictorial space and the surface of the canvas. These ideas of resolving visual conflicts by intuitive manipulation of color and tone formed the basis of Hofmann's teaching and were important in the development of the work of the Abstract Expressionists□

Hans Hofmann
Deep within the Ravine
1965
84⅛″ × 60⅜″
The Metropolitan Museum of Art

postcards, or color transparencies their starting point.

The straightforward reproduction of photographs in paint on canvas without any evidence of the artist's intervention has aroused much controversy. Richard Estes (b. 1936) is one of the major figures in this movement and his *Ansonia* (1977) is an example of this type of art. Estes' starting point is a color transparency, enlarged to show all the details. He then painstakingly copies this on to the canvas. In its overall clarity, with its lack of selective emphasis, his painting is close to that of Andrew Wyeth, though in his choice of subject matter – the empty city – there are stronger links with Edward Hopper. It is an art about perception. We do not perceive situations in this way – all details are not apparent to us at the same time and we tend to scan our environment, switching from one object to another in rapid succession. Estes' mechanical presentation

Jackson Pollock
Autumn Rhythm 1950
105″ × 207″
The Metropolitan Museum
of Art

*I*t would be wrong to see Realists and Regionalists of the 1930s and 1940s as being the sole representatives of the American social and political conscience in the visual arts during those decades. It is certainly arguable that the emergence of Abstract Expressionism in the 1940s was just as much a reaction to the dire social conditions of the 1930s and the direct trauma of the war years. Indeed the tension established between poetic harmony and physical violence which lies at the heart of Pollock's work reflects his life and times with great accuracy.

Pollock's early work was clearly related to the landscape and cultural traditions of the American West, and it is in the open epic possibilities suggested by the landscape, and in the rhythms and notations of American Indian art that his mature work took root.

Pollock's work remained closely locked to his perception of nature and natural forces, and spans the gap between external nature and the inner temperament of human nature □

of minutely detailed cityscapes forces us to look at those details that most people would never be aware of – the reflections of the buildings in the plate glass store window (reflections play an important part in his painting), the objects seen through the glass inside the store, the details of the plants and trees with every leaf visible and, most of all, the smooth surface of the canvas. Although realism is the vehicle, Estes' concerns are with the formal elements of the equilibrium and the ambiguity between the two-dimensional surface of the canvas and the three-dimensional illusion of pictorial space – a concern which has occupied artists since Cézanne and the beginnings of Modernism.

Abstract Art

For many people the inclusion of a section on abstract art in a book about landscapes of the United States may seem an anomaly, but one of the important points about considering art is that the gap between realism and abstraction which at times seems so wide is in other ways a small step and the similarities between realist and abstract art are greater than the differences. The work of artists such as O'Keeffe, Rauschenberg, Avery and Sheeler demonstrates these similarities and although the paintings shown in this section are not all inspired by landscapes there are, within their form and structure, elements which relate them to landscape painting and so justify their inclusion.

The immigration to the United States of German-born artists in the 1930s had a profound effect on the direction of American art. One of the most significant of these immigrants in this context was Hans Hofmann (1880–1966), a teacher as well as a painter who, through his teaching in the art school that he opened in New York, continued the theories that he had taught in Germany. The essence of these ideas was concerned with the effects of color on pictorial space and by adjusting colors and shapes in an intuitive way, the artist could arrive at an equilibrium between the surface of the canvas and the pictorial space. In some ways it was an extension of the work of Cézanne, whose paintings achieved a balance between the surface plane and the illusion of depth. His painting *Deep Within the Ravine* (1965) can be read, as the title suggests, as a landscape painted with strong gestural marks and simplified shapes.

Much of his work is more architectural, with rectangles of pure color, often overlapping, filling the surface of the canvas. The painterly quality of the surface remains strong in these works and it is this painterly approach, plus the intuitive reactions to constructing the image, that led via Hofmann's teaching to the development of Abstract Expressionism in the 1950s. This movement was not solely the result of Hofmann's teaching and the artistic and intellectual climate of New York played a vital role in its evolution, but many artists trained with Hofmann in New York and his teaching was fundamental to their originating a personal style.

The most famous exponent of Abstract Expressionism or Action Painting was Jackson Pollock (1912–56), who exhibited his first 'drip' paintings in 1948. These were created by Pollock dribbling and splashing paint on to large canvases laid out on the floor. The gestural marks are the results of the artist's actions, in effect a visual record of his movements, and the resulting surface is an interwoven complex of swirling linear strokes. The control exerted over this process is much greater than the layman imagines. These paintings aroused derision and outrage in the public, but for many younger artists they spoke of freedom and excitement. Jackson Pollock arrived at this personal style by a process which led him from figurative art through primitive art objects via the automatic writing of Surrealism and oriental calligraphy.

The contribution of the Works Progress Administration to the evolution of this style must not be underestimated for it brought together groups of artists and enabled them to develop their ideas free from the pressures of earning a living. It allowed Pollock to develop his ideas from the Expressionist tendencies of Thomas Hart Benton with whom he studied, and from the work of Ryder and the mural paintings of the 1930s which had some effect on the scale of his own mature images. The 'all-over' emphasis of marks created by Pollock in these works is a major innovation in handling pictorial space and yet antecedents can be found for this. Claude Monet's large Giverny paintings, with their subject of the lily ponds, are strikingly similar in their emphasis on total surface with expressive brushmarks and their lack of any clearly defined composition. Pollock had

Willem de Kooning
Door to the River 1960
80″ × 70″
Whitney Museum of
American Art, New York

*W*here Pollock's work is a harmonic, poetic whole, built up out of the violence of its constituent parts, de Kooning's pulls violence into the foreground of the painting. In doing this, the artist has also brought to our attention the shape and flow of the pigment on the surface of the canvas. There are similarities here with the work of Hofmann.

Much of de Kooning's work was, and remains, figurative in its basic references – he is noted for his series of female nude subjects – and it seems here that despite the clearly abstract motivations and outcome of the painting, de Kooning's composition retains a sense of the classic landscape articulation of horizontal distance and vertical foreground elements. The rectilinear direction of many of the brush

strokes reinforces this impression, and his clear reference to a landscape subject in the title points clearly to his own awareness of such a connection □

arrived by a different path at a point not too far distant from these late landscapes by Monet. As with Monet's vast paintings, the sheer size of the canvas becomes the spectator's environment, seeming to surround him, and where some of the Pop Artists such as Rauschenberg extended their paintings into the spectator's space by the addition of three-dimensional objects, these paintings attempt to break down the barriers between pictorial space and the real space of the viewer.

The quality which comes across most strongly in Pollock's painting is a sense of tranquillity; the marks might be generated by energy and spontaneity but the final tapestry of lines radiates an image of a harmonious, self-contained world as in *Autumn Rhythm (Number 30)* (1950). Not all Abstract Expressionist artists produced such serene images. Willem de Kooning (b. 1904) exhibits in his work a sense of violence. In the 1950s the subject of his paintings was the image of a woman, but a woman transformed by the slashing brushstrokes of de Kooning's expressionism. Just as Pollock's canvases are a record of physical actions of applying the paint, so do de Kooning's paintings show the vigor and vitality of his confrontation with the canvas.

De Kooning's work moves between figurative references and totally abstract images. *Door to the River* (1960) contains the representational landscape references of the title but it is so far removed from realism that it can be considered abstract. There are strong ties here with the approach of Hofmann in his manipulation of pigment on the surface, creating, destroying and recreating the image to reach the desired conclusion, but it rejects the rectilinear structure of much of Hofmann's work in favor of expressive intuitive statements. Like Hofmann's, de Kooning's influence was spread through teaching.

In 1933 Josef Albers fled from Germany when the Bauhaus was closed by the National Socialist Party and founded Black Mountain College in North Carolina. Just as the Bauhaus was the most revolutionary and influential art school in Europe in the late 1920s and early 1930s, so Black Mountain College achieved a similar status in the United States using the Bauhaus Basic Course.

The list of alumni and faculty at Black Mountain College reads like a *Who's Who* of famous New York artists of the fifties and sixties. De Kooning, Helen Frankenthaler, Robert Motherwell, Merce Cunningham and John Cage were also involved while Robert Rauschenberg and John Chamberlain were but two of the famous alumni.

Not all of the abstract art of the 1940s and 1950s was in the form of action painting. One of the most original painters to emerge in this period was Mark Rothko (1903–70), who rejected the aggressive surfaces of de Kooning, Kline and Pollock and presented thin veils of color interrelating within variations of a personal structure. The resulting image of atmospheric rectangular shapes setting up vibrations between themselves and the ground as in *Four Darks in Red* (1958) have strong links to the painterly tradition of much landscape painting. The division of the canvas into simple bands of color is strongly reminiscent of John Frederick Kensett's paintings as in *Passing Off of the Storm* (1872), even to the sensuous handling of the brushstrokes. Like Pollock's and de Kooning's, Rothko's early work was influenced by Surrealism, and took the form of totemic images, but whereas Pollock developed the use of linear marks, from this point Rothko began to explore simpler, less defined shapes in watercolor. The forms of the ground and sky behind his totemic images emerged to become the basis of his vocabulary of shapes.

Among the early Hudson River School painters such as Thomas Cole there was an attempt to show the nature of God through the glorification of his work by painting the untouched landscapes of the American continent. In Rothko there is also a strong spiritual content but it is the spiritualism of inner contemplation. Probably the closest links are with Luminism, but in Rothko the specific landscape references have been replaced by a distillation of light within a formal structure of indistinct rectangles. *Four Darks in Red* is from the period when his colors became darker and heavier, reflecting his personal mental turmoil which culminated in his suicide in 1970.

The poetic landscape suggestions inherent in the paintings of Mark Rothko contrast strongly with the 'landscape' imagery of Clyfford Still (1904–80). In Still's paintings there is a denseness of surface and a torn edge to the shapes which give the feeling of struggle in their creation. Still developed his style of painting in California where he taught at the California School of Fine Arts; he began to visit New York in the 1940s,

Mark Rothko
Four Darks in Red 1958
102″ × 116″
Whitney Museum of
American Art, New York

The broad sweep of Rothko's delicately textured color bands are immediately and intentionally reminiscent of landscape forms. Less intentional is their similarity to the Hudson River and the Luminist schools of painting, but the revelation of a spiritual reality by combining color and form on a grand scale is common to both Rothko and his nineteenth-century forebears. Obviously there any similarity rests, as the early painters were concerned with the glorification of nature as experienced in the exterior landscape; Rothko's landscape is that of the contemplative spirit. Rothko's paintings thus take the American Dream landscape in its spiritual/religious form to its natural conclusion – no longer 'figures in a landscape', but rather the landscape within all of us □

finally moving there for eleven years in 1950. His mature style was reached by 1947 – a 'landscape' of cliffs and towering forests with a strong vertical emphasis in the markmaking process. Just as connections can be made between Rothko's work and that of the Luminist painters so links can be seen in the vastness and drama of Still's painting to the panoramic views of Bierstadt and Moran. His images have a sense of violence and majesty with torn shapes constructing the actual surface as in *Untitled* (1957).

Clyfford Still had strong beliefs; he rejected all European Art for its decadence and sterility and believed in the power of his painting to reflect the fundamentals of the universe, a concept that he shared with some of the Hudson River School. His paintings

*C*lyfford Still's color field paintings do not reach as far out as Rothko's, and in their incipient violence and trauma find a middle ground between the contemplative and the active, between Rothko and, say, Pollock. But once again we enter the twilight world where the received image of the Romantic American landscape as conceived by artists from Cole to Bierstadt is reformulated as an expression of internal landscapes.

The process inevitably involves cutting out extraneous detail – the peripheral mass of perceived, visual experience – in order to get closer to universal, ineffable truths. As in the work of de Kooning, Still makes us aware of his own process of creation in building up the surface of the painting in impasto streaks of pigment, indeed pushing the context of the painting off the canvas into our real space. Still's careful juxtaposition of color allows him to deny any sense of pictorial space or depth, once again forcing the picture into our world, rather than allowing it to recede into its own compartmentalized universe □

Clyfford Still
Untitled 1957
112″ × 154″
Whitney Museum of
American Art, New York

are built up with thick pigment laid on with a palette knife creating a heavy, tactile texture which emphasized the actual surface of the canvas. By making the shapes and the ground indivisible in his painting he eliminates any sense of pictorial space.

Landscapes in diverse forms continued to be painted, from photorealist images to Expressionist post-modern statements and abstract works with landscape connotations. The breaking down of boundaries which Marcel Duchamp began with his exhibition of the urinal in New York in 1917 continued through the twentieth century, giving rise in the fifties and sixties to performance art – a union of art, music and drama. Developments in landscape broke new boundaries with the work of artists such as Robert Smithson

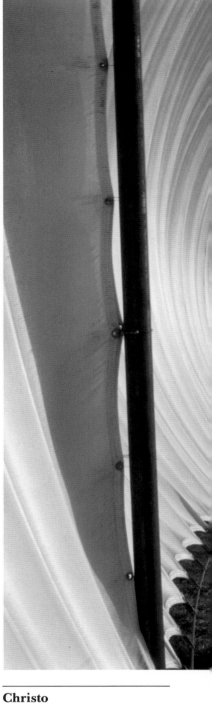

(1938–1973) in the movement known as land art. These are statements made with the physical landscape where art is no longer a marketable product, a painting to be hung on a wall or a sculpture to be installed in a building. Most of these works have a short life span and involve many assistants and machines to construct them. Smithson's *Spiral Jetty* (1970) is the result of moving large amounts of soil and rock into the Great Salt Lake in Utah to form a spiral of land linked to the edge of the lake. Many of these works are in inaccessible or rarely visited places so that the potential audience is not a major consideration. The monumentality of many of these works recalls prehistoric ritual structures and their primeval nature contrasts oddly with the machinery used to create them. For the Hudson River School, the attraction of unexploited landscape was one of reflecting the presence of God, the creator of all things. Here, however, we see landscape physically transformed; man becomes the creator of his own landscape.

Christo (Jaracheff, b. 1935) is well-known as the artist who wraps up objects – a motorbike, a bridge, a stretch of the Australian coastline. By wrapping the landscape he transforms it so that it takes on the quality of mystery reminiscent of Surrealist works such as Man Ray's wrapped sewing machine of 1920. In hanging an enormous curtain called *Valley Curtain, Rifle Colorado* (1970–72) he is making a comment about the scale and shape of that specific place, as well as promoting an awareness of the surrounding landscape. Some of his projects are unrealized – they remain as drawings, models and photomontages, his sole source of income for these often massive undertakings. The models and photographs are also the only record of his projects. The size and complexity of these operations mean years of lobbying and complicated financing and the scale of them can be understood by the example of his project to surround the Islands of Biscayne Bay, which was carried out at a cost of over $3,500,000. His *Running Fence* created an 18 ft high curtained fence across the state of California, dividing Sonoma and Marin counties with its 24½-mile (39-kilometre) structure. As in many twentieth-century works scale is an important factor. However, this tradition stretches back over centuries and can be seen in some of the prehistoric earthworks in South America, the size of which is such that they also cannot be seen in their entirety by a man on the ground.

Many of the artists connected with this kind of image are concerned with the process of social interaction and the tools of planning and negotiation. The process becomes the art form; organizing and acquiring permission, negotiating with lawyers and state and federal governments, the raising of funds, the enlisting of assistants – all this takes many months and this political and social comment becomes a major part of the artistic statement.

The ambiguities about the nature of art within these manifestations are not a new phenomenon. Questions about perception and definitions fill the galleries of twentieth-

Christo
Running Fence, Sonoma and Marin Counties, California 1972–76
24½ miles long × 18 feet high
Christo, 1976 photo
Wolfgang Volz

Robert Smithson
Spiral Jetty 1970
Gianfranco Gorgoni/
Contact/Colorific!

*T*he American urge to find a national cultural and even personal
identity in the landscape of the New World has led its
inhabitants, not unnaturally, to become actively involved in
transforming that landscape. The roots of this urge probably lie in
the empire-building vision of the great railroad builders and prairie
farmers, pushing tracks of steel across the land, and turning the
prairie grass under the plowshare. This urge has taken many forms,
from the monumental reliefs of Mount Rushmore to the patchwork
quilting of the Midwest farms. Environmentalists and satellite
surveys have brought home to us the impact of mankind's activities
on the landscape around us, and in America that process has been
more rapid, and often more spectacular, than in any other region of
the world. The appearance of Land and Earth Art in the 1960s and
1970s related to many concerns – some of them traditional, looking
back to the vast ancient land sculptures of the Nazca Valley in Peru,
some of them sensationalistic, such as Christo's wrapping projects.
Robert Smithson remains the archetypal earth artist, his Spiral
Jetty posing an enigmatic, man-made question mark in the barren
waters of Salt Lake, Utah.

Christo's work is avowedly spectacular, and takes the landscape
on its own terms. His work is less that of an Earth artist, and is
more closely related to Happenings on the one hand, and the
tradition of monumental architecture and engineering on the other.
The Running Fence project was meticulously documented at all
stages, from the original negotiations for temporary land rights,
through construction contracts and material supplies, to the
technical logistics of erecting the fence itself. The legal, financial,
social and technical aspects of the project represented a very major
aspect of its significance as a Happening.

On an aesthetic level Christo is concerned to make us ask
questions about the way in which his contribution to an object or
landscape has altered our perception of it. But the undeniable
impact of the Running Fence was as a monumental engineering
feat: 'I want to present something that we never saw before. . . not
an image but a real thing like the pyramids of Egypt or the Great
Wall of China' □

century art and none more so than in the work of Jasper Johns (b. 1930) in his paintings of the American flag, targets and maps. Within the context of landscape Johns has taken a map of the United States and painted it freely in primary colors applied with strong gestural marks in an Abstract Expressionist mode. He has then superimposed, by the use of stencils, the names of the states, some of which are partially obscured by further painting as in *Map* (1961). It is a comment and a question about the paradox that arises between the diagram – the map – and the fine art tradition – the painterly treatment.

Jasper Johns
Map 1961
Oil on canvas
6'6" × 10'3"
Museum of Modern Art, New York

We have moved from an art of perception to an art of conception. All landscape art is the product of our method of study or, as Heisenberg said, 'What we observe is not nature itself but nature exposed to our method of questioning.' What we are concerned with is the ever-changing mode of questioning. It is not possible to predict how this will evolve over the remainder of this century, but whether easel painting continues or disappears under the weight of computer-generated images it is certain that the rural and urban environments of the United States will continue to inspire American artists.

Washington, DC, in 1944 and a retrospective exhibition of his work was held at the Whitney Museum of American Art in 1960, five years before his death.

GEORGE WESLEY BELLOWS 1882–1925

Born in Columbus, Ohio, Bellows graduated from Ohio State University and continued studying at New York School of Art under Robert Henri and Kenneth Hayes Miller. After his election as an associate of the National Academy of Design in 1909, he set up his studio in New York near the athletic club which provided source material for his painting of prize fights.

Bellows taught at the Art Students League and exhibited six paintings in the 1913 Armory Show. By 1916 he had begun to work in lithography, producing images based on the First World War, reminiscent of Goya. He joined the Society of Independent Artists founded by John Sloan in 1917.

THOMAS HART BENTON 1889–1975

Born in Neosho, Missouri, into a political family. His father was a member of Congress and introduced Benton to the art world of Washington, DC. In 1908 he visited Paris, the birthplace of avant-garde development, but Benton was not sympathetic to these new ideas. After his return to America, he traveled widely within the country, drawing from the American scene subjects which he was to use in his Regionalist paintings.

His mural series of the 1930s show his rejection of Modernism and the promotion of his Regionalist message with its emphasis on rural activities and its disapproval of city life. During the Second World War he produced the *Perils of War*, a series illustrating the dangers of the age, but by the 1950s he had gradually abandoned social comment in his paintings.

Thomas Hart Benton

ARTISTS' BIOGRAPHIES

WASHINGTON ALLSTON 1779–1843

Born in Georgetown, South Carolina. Following his graduation from Harvard, Allston traveled to London in 1801, where he was admitted to the Royal Academy School under the presidency of his fellow countryman, Benjamin West. Here he was attracted to the romantic paintings of Henry Fuseli. In the company of John Vanderlyn, he subsequently went to Paris via the Netherlands and studied the paintings in the Louvre, collected by Napoleon. Allston lived in Rome from 1804–8, where he studied and painted from the Great Masters with an international group of artists and writers including Coleridge and Wordsworth.

Allston returned to Boston, remaining there until his second visit to England in 1811, where he achieved some success as a history painter. On his return to America, he was elected an honorary member of the American Academy of Fine Arts.

MILTON AVERY 1885–1965

Born at Sand Bank (later Altmar), New York, he moved with his family to Wilson Station, Connecticut. Avery worked as a filing clerk and in various other positions until 1924. During this time he studied at the Connecticut League of Art Students in Hartford. He exhibited some of his work in 1915.

Avery moved to New York City in 1925 and married Sally Michel, another artist, the following year. At this point he enrolled at the Art Students League, where he remained until 1938. During this time some of his work was exhibited in the 1927 Independents Show and from 1930 onwards his work showed a strong Fauvist influence.

With the support of his wife, he began to paint full time in 1938 and was employed in the Federal Art Project of the Works Progress Administration. His first one-man show was held in

ALBERT BIERSTADT 1830–1902

Born in Solingen, Germany, Bierstadt emigrated with his family to America where they settled in New Bedford, Massachusetts. In 1853 he visited Germany where he studied at the Düsseldorf Academy, then he traveled through Switzerland to Italy, where he continued his training in Rome. His companions included Worthington Whittredge and Sanford Gifford.

On his return to the US he exhibited at the National Academy of Design. In 1859–60 he accompanied the expedition of Colonel Frederick W Lander to survey a route through the Rocky Mountains and traveled to the White Mountains. These provided inspiration for paintings which he executed on his return from the West. When he exhibited *Rocky Mountains, Lander's Peak* in New York, it brought him instant fame. Later the Legion of Honor was awarded to him by Napoleon III. But by 1880 his reputation began to decline, accompanied by several misfortunes including the destruction of his Hudson mansion, the death of his wife and bankruptcy.

GEORGE CALEB BINGHAM 1811–1879

Born in Augusta County, Virginia, Bingham moved in 1819 to Missouri, where he spent most of his life. He started work as a sign painter for a cabinetmaker and turned from sign painting to portrait painting in 1833. He studied art for a few months in Philadephia where he discovered the interest Easterners had in the West. When he moved back West he began to produce his river scenes. His reputation became widespread when the American Art Union issued his engraving of the *Jolly Flatboatmen* to its 10,000 subscribers.

Bingham became involved in politics, serving in the Missouri State Legislature, as well as acting as State Treasurer and Adjutant General at various times. But throughout this period he continued to produce paintings featuring his two favourite subjects, the American West and politics.

RALPH ALBERT BLAKELOCK 1847–1919

Born in New York City, Blakelock was largely self-taught. His earliest work exhibited at the National Academy of Design reflects the influence of both the Hudson River School and the Barbizon School. He traveled to the West of America and the sketches he made among the Indians became the starting point for his imagined lyrical landscapes.

He married in 1877 but by 1891 had his first mental breakdown, caused by the difficulty of supporting a large family. He was committed to an asylum in 1899 as a result of another breakdown and he remained there for 17 years. He was then transfered to a hospital in New Jersey and while there was elected to the National Academy of Design. In July of 1919 he was taken from the asylum by his legal guardian and seemed to have recovered. Sadly he died one month after his release.

OSCAR BLUEMNER 1867–1938

Born in Hanover, Germany, Bluemner studied to be an architect, but also painted portraits. He emigrated to the United States in 1892 and practiced as an architect in New York.

George Catlin

In addition to exhibiting in the Armory Show of 1913, Bleumner was also a participant in shows at Stieglitz's 291 Gallery. He also took part in the Forum Exhibition of 1916. In the 1920s and 1930s his work developed from the earlier Cubist-influenced style towards an abstract style.

KARL BODMER 1809–1893

Born in Riesbach, Switzerland, Bodmer was hired by Prince Maximilian von Wied-Neuwied to be resident artist for his exploration of the American West. The expedition arrived at St Louis in 1833 and proceeded by steamboat and by keelboat upriver to Fort McKenzie. Bodmer's drawings of Indian scenes are among the finest documentary evidence of Indian life. At the end of the expedition, Bodmer returned to Europe and settled in Barbizon where he did the illustrations for the Prince's journal.

He exhibited paintings in the Paris Salon, work that was produced with Barbizon painters such as Millet and Rousseau. He never returned to the US but continued to paint landscapes and produce illustrations for books and magazines.

GEORGE CATLIN 1796–1872

Born in Wilkes-Barre, Pennsylvania, Catlin practiced law until 1821 when his interest turned to art. Inspired by seeing a delegation of Indians passing through Philadelphia he decided to record them and their lifestyle in the West.

Catlin's vast collection of paintings was exhibited in New York then taken by him on tour to Baltimore, Philadelphia, Boston and Washington, DC. He offered this Gallery of Indian Paintings to the US government but it was unwilling to buy. He also traveled to England and France with his exhibition of paintings and Indian show. He was jailed for his debts in 1852 but released by the sale of his paintings to Joseph Harrison.

Catlin produced a second collection of paintings of Indian tribes which was finally accepted by the Smithsonian in 1879.

Christo

WILLIAM MERRITT CHASE 1849–1916

Born in Williamsburg (now Nineveh), Indiana, Chase first studied art with Benjamin Hayes, a portrait painter in Indianapolis. He moved to New York City to study at the National Academy of Design, then studied at the Royal Academy in Munich. During his stay in this city, he shared a studio with fellow artist Frank Duvenick, who was instrumental in importing the Munich style with its bravura brushwork to the United States. After a brief stay in Venice, Chase returned to New York to teach at the Art Students League.

His meeting with James McNeill Whistler in London prompted him to lighten his palette from the somber tones of the Munich School. The Chase School was founded by him in 1896 and he taught there until 1908. During this time he joined the Ten American Painters group.

CHRISTO (CHRISTO JARACHEFF) 1935–

Born in Gabrova, Bulgaria, Christo was a student at the Academy of Fine Arts in Sofia, and he subsequently spent one term at the Academy of Fine Arts in Vienna. He moved to Paris where he was a cofounder of the *Nouveaux Réalités* group. Here he started to evolve the art form which was to make him famous – the package. His first one dates from around 1958. The size of these works grew from small wrapped packages to large objects, to buildings and to landscapes.

After six years in Paris he moved to New York with his wife Jeanne-Claude who takes an active part in his projects.

FREDERIC EDWIN CHURCH 1826–1900

Born in Hartford, Connecticut, to a wealthy family who allowed him to pursue his interest in art, Church became a pupil of Thomas Cole, the leading painter of the Hudson River School.

Church moved to New York where he established a studio and became a member of the National Academy of Design.

In the late 1840s he traveled throughout New York and New England, making sketches which he then developed into paintings, and these sold well. In 1853, with his friend Cyrus Field, he made an expedition to South America, making sketches and drawings from which he produced paintings shown in 1855. These paintings established his reputation.

His travels also took him to Maine, New Hampshire, and Vermont and Niagara Falls. *Niagara* and *Heart of the Andes* established him as a major painter both in America and in Europe. He traveled extensively in Europe and the Middle East, gathering information which he translated into paintings. During the later part of his life he produced many small oil sketches of the region around Olana (his villa on the Hudson) and of Mexico, where he spent most winters from 1882.

THOMAS COLE 1801–1848

Born in Lancashire, England, Cole trained as an engraver of woodblocks in Liverpool. He moved with his family to America in 1818 where he continued engraving for the textile trade. He studied art with an itinerant painter and, inspired by the portraits of his teacher, started work as a portrait painter, then turned to landscape. He eventually studied at the Pennsylvania Academy of Fine Arts. After moving to New York in 1825 Cole's paintings of the Hudson Valley brought him into the circle of prominent artists of the city. He was elected to the National Academy of Design.

He visited Europe where he met John Constable and JMW Turner and exhibited at the Royal Academy. Cole continued his Grand Tour to Paris and Italy where he admired the romanticism of the Italian landscape. In addition to his paintings he recorded his ideas in writing: he produced essays, poems and thoughts on the American landscape. Frederick E Church became his pupil shortly before Cole died.

SAMUEL COLMAN 1832–1920

Born in Portland, Maine, the son of a wealthy book dealer and publisher, Colman moved to New York while still a child. As a pupil of Asher B Durand he exhibited some work at the National Academy of Design. His paintings of the White Mountains, Lake George and other Hudson River scenes brought him early recognition and he was elected associate member of the National Academy of Design.

Colman made a Grand Tour of Europe from 1860 to 1862 and on his return to the US he became a full academician. He produced a series of paintings of wagon trains as a result of his trip to the American West. He wrote two books on art and collaborated with Tiffany on several design projects.

JASPER FRANCIS CROPSEY 1823–1900

Born in Staten Island, New York, Cropsey was awarded a diploma by the New York Mechanics Institute and became apprenticed to the architect Joseph Trench. Edward Maury, an English artist, gave Cropsey watercolor lessons and he also took classes in life drawing at the National Academy of Design. He eventually opened his own architectural business in New York but by 1845 he was painting landscapes full time. He taught at New York City Studio and completed paintings from sketches he had made on his travels to Europe. But he also turned to the American landscape, working in the White Mountains, Greenwood Lake and the Hudson River Valley, his paintings showing the influence of Thomas Cole and Asher B Durand.

On his second visit to London he produced paintings of autumnal landscapes, such as *Autumn on the Hudson*, which established him in London society and his reputation followed him back to America, bringing financial rewards. He continued to paint Hudson River-type landscapes, many in watercolor, even after they declined in popularity.

JOHN STEUART CURRY 1897–1946

Born in Dunavent, Kansas, Curry worked as an illustrator for five years before going to Paris for a year. His painting *Baptism in Kansas*, illustrating the religious rites of a rural community, established his reputation and other paintings depicting scenes from rural life in the Midwest followed.

He became the leading artist of the Regionalists, a group which included Thomas Hart Benton and Grant Wood. In 1936, Curry was appointed Professor of Art at the University of Wisconsin. His major work was a series of murals which he painted for the state capital in Topeka, Kansas.

STUART DAVIS 1894–1964

Born in Philadelphia, Davis left high school to study under Robert Henri for three years. He exhibited with the Eight and other artists rejected by the National Academy in the Indepen-

Stuart Davis

Willem de Kooning

dents Show. The Armory Show in which Davis exhibited work introduced him to the European Modernists, who eventually had a profound effect on his subsequent work. The *Eggbeater* series show his experiments with Modernism.

Davis visited Paris for two years in 1928 and produced paintings derived from the Paris street scenes rendered in an abstract form. During the 1930s he was employed by the Federal Art Project of the Works Progress Administration and developed his abstract landscape style. A retrospective of his work was held at the Museum of Modern Art in 1945. From the 1950s onwards references to objects in his paintings became more fragmented and more abstract.

WILLEM DE KOONING 1904–

Born in Rotterdam, de Kooning studied at the Akademie voor Beeldende Kunsten en Technischen Wetenschappen, Amsterdam, while he worked as an apprentice commercial decorator. In 1927 he emigrated to the US as a stowaway on a ship and worked as a house painter in Hoboken, New Jersey. He eventually moved to New York where he worked in various commercial jobs and became acquainted with Arshile Gorky and Stuart Davis. Gorky and de Kooning shared a studio and under his influence de Kooning began to experiment with abstraction. The 1930s also saw him working on murals for the Federal Art Project of the Works Progress Administration, including one for the New York World's Fair in 1939.

His first exhibition was held in 1948 at the Charles Egan gallery in New York and at the same time he became an instructor at Black Mountain College, which was run at that time by Josef Albers.

De Kooning's figure paintings of the 1940s and 1950s were superseded in the late 1950s by a move to abstraction, linking him with the Abstract Expressionist movement. His early training encouraged a practical approach which he used in the 1970s to produce expressionistic figurative sculpture.

CHARLES DEMUTH 1883–1935

Born in Lancaster, Pennsylvania, Demuth studied at the Pennsylvania Academy of Fine Arts. He visited Europe on several occasions and on his second visit, which lasted two years, he absorbed the ideas of the Fauve painters in Paris and also the structural approach of Cézanne. His landscapes of this period combine Cubist analysis with a freer Expressionist brushwork. Several styles are apparent in his work of this time, each style being determined by a different subject matter. Industrial landscapes appear as important subjects in his paintings with the emergence of his Precisionist style.

THOMAS DOUGHTY 1793–1856

Born in Philadelphia, Doughty spent his early years working as an apprentice to a leather currier. In 1820, he started painting, specializing in landscapes depicting scenes from the Pennsylvania, New York and New England countryside. He was elected a member of the Pennsylvania Academy and had his first major exhibition in New York at the National Academy of Design in 1826. He also published several illustrated books in partnership with his brother.

From 1837 until 1846 he made several journeys to Europe, visiting England, Ireland and France. His landscapes after his English trip show the influence of John Constable.

ARTHUR G DOVE 1880–1946

Born in Canandaigua, New York, Dove worked as an illustrator for magazines. He visited France where he absorbed the influence of the paintings of Paul Cézanne, and this is reflected in his still-life and landscape works of this period. But by 1910 Modernism appeared in the six abstract paintings that he produced on his return to New York. Having established an abstract style, Dove maintained it for the rest of his life with very little variation in it. Some of his late work reflects his illness with his use of somber colors.

ASHER BROWN DURAND 1796–1886

Born in Jefferson Village (now Maplewood), New Jersey, Durand became apprenticed to engraver Peter Maverick, whom he joined as a partner in the engraving business for three years.

The acceptance of a commission to engrave *The Declaration of Independence* for John Trumbull precipitated a split in the partnership but completion of the commission in 1823 established Durand as the leading engraver in the country. He started to move towards painting, producing portraits then landscapes in the 1830s. He went with Thomas Cole on a sketching tour to the Adirondacks which encouraged him to concentrate on landscape painting. Durand embarked on a Grand Tour of Europe with John W Casilear and John F Kensett in 1840–1.

Later on he spent summers sketching in the Adirondacks, the Catskills and the White Mountains, and used these detailed studies for his subsequent paintings. On the death of Cole he was recognized as the leader of the Hudson River School and of American landscape painting.

THOMAS EAKINS 1844–1916

Born in Philadelphia, Eakins attended classes at the Pennsylvania Academy of Fine Arts and also studied anatomy at Jefferson Medical College. This combination of art and science runs throughout his career. In 1866, Eakins went to Paris, spending three years at the Ecole des Beaux Arts where he was strongly influenced by the academic training. During the 1870s he produced many paintings of rowers, showing his interest in mathematical perspective in the many preliminary drawings. He later produced paintings of landscapes with figures and also turned to portraits which showed great insight. He did not achieve wide acclaim until after his death, perhaps because his whole approach to art was very unconventional and unfashionable to the general art audience of the day.

RALPH EARL 1751–1801

Born in Worcester County, Massachusetts, Earl moved with his family to Leicester, Massachusetts, where he spent his early years. His loyalist tendencies forced him to flee to England where he studied with Benjamin West and Sir Joshua Reynolds and also exhibited his work at the Royal Academy. On his return to America, he continued to paint portraits, many of which are interesting because of the integration of the landscape background with the figure. He was a popular portraitist in Connecticut up until his death.

RICHARD ESTES 1936–

Born in Keewane, Illinois, Estes attended the Art Institute of Chicago, after which he worked as an illustrator in publishing and advertising in Evanston, Illinois. He moved to Spain in 1962 and began painting there. From 1966 onwards he devoted himself to painting full time.

Estes had his first one-man show at the Allan Stone Gallery in New York and has exhibited regularly with them and with other galleries in the US. His painting derives closely from photographs which are at first sight merely copied. In the painting process, selection takes place and the resulting image is an abstraction from the original material.

LYONEL FEININGER 1871–1956

Born in New York, the son of a German immigrant musician, Feininger studied the violin. Having left America for Germany at the age of 16 to continue his violin studies, he enrolled in the School of Decorative Arts in Hamburg while waiting for a place at the Berlin Academy. In Hamburg he studied drawing, and then he worked as an illustrator in Berlin for newspapers and reviews. A visit to Paris encouraged him to paint and during a subsequent visit to Paris he encountered Cubism and began to explore and develop a personal style. Back in Berlin he produced his first Constructivist composition. In 1919, he became a teacher at the Bauhaus in Weimar. He returned to the US before the Second World War.

His work is dominated by a strong linear structure related to Cubism and to Futurism and this continued to be one of his characteristics throughout his career.

WILLIAM GLACKENS 1870–1938

Born in Philadelphia, Pennsylvania. While a reporter for the *Philadelphia Press* Glackens met Robert Henri who persuaded him to paint rather then merely illustrate. Henri remained a major influence on his life. Glackens studied at the Pennsylvania Academy of Fine Arts with John Sloan, George Luks and Everett Shinn. In the company of Robert Henri he went to Paris and exhibited at the Salon. On his return he took another appointment as a reporter/illustrator in New York, and continued painting. When the work of his colleagues was rejected by the Academy, they decided to form a group called the Eight, to exhibit in the Macbeth Gallery.

Glackens helped with the organization of the Independents Show and took a major part in the Armory Show as chairman of the selection committee for American art. In 1917 he was elected the first president of the Society of Independent Artists.

FRANCIS GUY 1760–1820

Born in the Lake District, England, Guy worked as a tailor in London. He emigrated to America and continued this occupation in Philadelphia and New York, but in 1798 he moved to Baltimore and turned to painting landscapes. His most famous paintings were of snow scenes showing small towns and their inhabitants. These are rendered with great precision which he achieved by the use of a perspective screen.

William Glackens

ALVAN FISHER 1792–1863

Born in Needham, Massachusetts and growing up in Dedham, Fisher received his first painting instruction from John Penniman. He turned from portraits to rural scenes which were financially more rewarding but eventually returned to portrait painting. He worked in many cities, including Charleston, South Carolina, and Hartford, Connecticut.

In 1825, he began a Grand Tour of Europe and spent some time studying in Paris. On his return to the US he settled in Boston, where he is reputed to have been the first Boston artist to paint landscapes. Fisher was financially successful in his painting career and in spite of losing his entire savings in 1835 he was able to recover and rebuild his resources.

SANFORD ROBINSON GIFFORD 1823–1880

Born in Greenfield, New York, Gifford grew up in Hudson and studied at Brown University for two years. He went to New York where he continued his studies under John Rubens Smith, who taught him perspective and anatomy. After sketching trips to the Catskills and the Berkshires and influenced by the landscapes of Thomas Cole, he moved from portraiture to landscapes. On the strength of his landscapes he was elected an associate member of the National Academy of Design and three years later became an Academician. He traveled to England, Scotland, Wales and France, continuing his Grand Tour in the company of Worthington Whittredge and ending up in Rome.

With John Kensett he went to the West in 1870 but was not seduced by the grandeur of the landscape. Instead he continued to try to find ways of depicting the quality of light. He achieved his effects by applying layers of varnish and transparent glazes of pigment.

MARSDEN HARTLEY 1877–1943

Born in Lewiston, Maine, Hartley had his first exhibition of black landscapes at Alfred Stieglitz's 291 Gallery. With some financial assistance from Stieglitz, he visited Europe where he came under the influence of the Cubists in Paris. In Munich he was attracted to the Expressionism of Franz Marc and Wassily Kandinsky. He started painting his abstractions which were exhibited with the Blaue Reiter group in Berlin. These were strongly in the style of Modernism, unlike the prevailing style which was strongly indebted to Cubism. His primary source of inspiration was the landscape of New Mexico and New England, which he depicted in simplified shapes with strong color.

FREDERICK CHILDE HASSAM 1859–1935

Born in Dorchester, Massachusetts. Hassam was apprenticed to a wood engraver in Boston, and started work as an illustrator. He studied in Paris for a time.

He eventually settled in New York, started to paint in an Impressionist style and began his summer painting trips to New England. His work at this time was strongly influenced by Monet. He taught at the Art Students League and was a founder member of the Ten American Painters, a group of painters who were inspired in some way by Impressionism.

Hassam exhibited in the Armory Show in New York. He remained an Impressionist painter throughout his life though his later work became more decorative and rather mannered. During his lifetime he gained great acclaim for his work and was the closest of all US painters to French Impressionism.

MARTIN JOHNSON HEADE 1819–1904

Born in Lumberville, Pennsylvania. Heade's early training was with Thomas Hicks. He traveled widely in Europe, studying in England, France and Italy, and two years of the time he was away from the US were spent in Rome.

When he returned to America he set up studios in various American cities – St Louis, Chicago, Trenton, returning to New York in 1859. This marked the beginning of his personal style with its concentration on the subtle atmospheric effects on landscape. His most memorable work dates from the 1860s to the 1880s and shows landscape views of New England which capture the effects of nature in his familiar horizontal format. On his marriage in 1883 he settled in Florida.

ROBERT HENRI 1865–1929

Born Robert Henri Cozad in Cincinnati, Ohio. His family moved to Nebraska where his father shot a man, forcing the family to flee first to Denver and then to Atlantic City. During this period the family was forced to live under assumed names and from this time on Robert's name was changed to Robert Henri. He received his first art training at the Pennsylvania Academy under Thomas Anschutz.

His next move was to the Académie Julian and the Ecole des Beaux Arts in Paris. Back in Philadelphia he met the newspaper illustrators Sloan, Glackens, Luks and Shinn who were to become with Henri the Ash Can School. With Glackens he went to France, Holland and Belgium in 1895. At this time he exhibited at the Paris Salon. In Paris he encountered the work of the French Impressionists and rejected it.

On his return to the US he settled in New York, where he was joined by his newspaper friends from Philadelphia. Henri began teaching at the Chase School but disenchantment with the prevailing attitudes prompted him to open his own school in 1909. The rejection of some of the work of his friends by the National Academy caused him to withdraw his own work and triggered the exhibition of the Eight at the Macbeth Gallery, at which they earned the title Ash Can School. He helped to organize the Independents Show, the first non-juried show in the US. His major contribution was as a teacher and he encouraged many artists to devote themselves full time to painting; some of his most famous students included Edward Hopper, Rockwell Kent and Stuart Davis.

EDWARD HICKS 1780–1849

Born in Attleborough (now Langhorne), Pennsylvania, Hicks, at the age of thirteen, was apprenticed to a coachmaker. He joined the Society of Friends – the Quakers – and married Sarah Worstall, settling in Milford, Pennsylvania. By this time he was a junior partner in the coachmaking business.

In 1811 he moved to Newtown where he stayed for the remainder of his life. In addition to his work in the coachmaking business, Hicks began to paint, decorating household objects and trade and tavern signs. Gradually he started painting landscapes and this led to his subject paintings, such as the *Peaceable Kingdom* of which there are over sixty versions. He became a Quaker minister and traveled extensively while painting. From his late period came his paintings of the residences of gentlemen.

Hans Hofmann

HANS HOFMANN 1880–1966

Born in Weissenberg, Bavaria, Hofmann studied in Munich and acquired a neo-Impressionist art training. He lived in Paris for a time where he became friends with many of the avant-garde artists of Cubism, Fauvism and Orphism, and founded an art school in Munich. He emigrated to the USA in 1932, gave courses in art at the University of California, and taught at the Art Students League in New York. He founded the Hans Hofmann School in New York and the Summer School in Provincetown. These two institutions lasted until 1958 when he closed them to concentrate on his own work.

One of the major developments of twentieth-century painting owes much to the painting and to the teaching of Hofmann; this movement was Abstract Expressionism. His contact with the avant-garde of Paris in the early years of the century strongly influenced his painting. Their ideas were synthesized and evolved into his own style in which gesture and directness were vital to the final structure. These characteristics were taken up by fellow artists such as Jackson Pollock.

WINSLOW HOMER 1836–1901

Born in Boston, Massachusetts, Homer was apprenticed to a lithographer. He worked as a freelance illustrator, contributing to *Harper's Weekly* and other publications, until he moved to New York and studied at the National Academy of Design. *Harper's Weekly* commissioned him to cover the Civil War. In 1866, he visited France and exhibited some of his work at the Exposition Universelle.

He settled in Tynemouth, England, in 1881–2 revisiting the US in the winter. In Tynemouth he became fascinated by the sea and the many drawings and watercolors that he produced here were used by him for later paintings.

On his return to the US he settled in Prout's Neck, Maine, where he painted the sea. During the winter he often went to the West Indies or to Florida but always returned to his secluded lifestyle in Maine in the summer.

EDWARD HOPPER 1882–1967

Born in Nyack, New York, where he lived for most of his life, Hopper's first studies were at the Correspondence School of Illustrating in New York. He then went on to the New York School of Art to study under Robert Henri, the leader of the Ash Can School, with William Merritt Chase, the Impressionist, and Kenneth Hayes Miller, who taught most of the Urban Realists of the 1930s. After working as an illustrator for a year he visited Paris in 1907, where he absorbed some of the current French ideas about depicting light.

He took part in the first exhibition of the Independent Artists. While supporting himself with commercial art he traveled around New England painting and also returned to France. He took part in the Armory Show and continued to exhibit his work while carrying on with his illustrating. The success of a show of watercolors in 1924 allowed him to devote himself full time to painting. The loneliness of city life became one of his major subjects, with empty streets or the inclusion of solitary figures.

In all these it is the light which is the most important element. A retrospective exhibition of his work was held at the Whitney Museum of American Art in 1950 and he was one of four artists chosen to represent the USA at the Venice Biennale.

GEORGE INNESS 1825–1894

Born near Newburgh, New York, Inness started work as an apprentice map engraver with the firm of Sherman and Smith in New York. His first art training was with the French painter, Régis Gignoux, in Brooklyn and he also came under the influence of the Hudson River School, especially Thomas Cole and Asher B Durand.

In 1847 he visited England and Italy to study the Old Masters and a second trip to Europe took him to Paris where he met the Barbizon painters, whose ideas and approaches to painting are reflected in his painting at this time. His work in the 1860s and 1870s showed the influence of both the Hudson River School and his European contacts, particularly the work of Claude Lorraine. His late work shows his arrival at solutions close to Impressionism despite the fact that he was not sympathetic to the Impressionists' aims.

Edward Hopper

which provided material for many of his paintings of the 1870s and 1880s. During the Civil War years he produced a series of paintings of the struggle between the North and the South and eventually turned to rural scenes of American life, producing what is regarded as some of his best work. His late work consists almost entirely of commissioned portraits.

JOHN KANE 1860–1934

Born in West Calder, Scotland. At the age of 19 Kane emigrated to the US, settling first in Pittsburgh where he started work as a laborer for the railroad. He mined coal in Alabama, Tennessee and Kentucky and also became involved in prize fighting. To be close to his family who had followed him from Scotland he moved back to Braddock, Pennsylvania, where he continued to work as a miner. It was at this time that he started to sketch from his surroundings.

At the age of 31 he lost his left leg in an accident on the railroad and after leaving hospital he became a watchman for the railroad. He married and during the following years he worked as a painter of railroad cars; during his lunch breaks he would paint landscapes on the sides of the cars, which he would then paint over when he resumed work.

The death of his only son in 1904 was an intense blow and he took to drinking heavily. After his wife left he became an itinerant worker. His interest in painting continued and he worked on scraps of wood, none of which is known to survive. The acceptance of a painting for the Carnegie International Exhibition in 1927 brought him into the limelight of the art world, and for the next seven years his work was included in all Carnegie International Exhibitions.

Jasper Johns

JASPER JOHNS 1930–

Born in Allendale, South Carolina. After a period of study at the University of South Carolina, Johns went to New York where he supported himself as a window decorator. From 1955 on he developed his major images of targets, flags and stenciled letters and numbers. It was a reaction to the current style of Abstract Expressionism which prevailed in New York. His show in 1958 at the Leo Castelli Gallery thrust him into instant stardom. Gradually he moved to a more expressionistic style while retaining the ready-made imagery.

His art is an art of paradox; a painting of a flag is not merely a representation of a flag but there is a concern with the actual surface qualities of the canvas. It is painting in the fine art tradition. From the 1960s on he began to attach real objects to the canvas, exploring further and developing the concepts of perception and representation.

JOHN FREDERICK KENSETT 1816–1872

Born in Cheshire, Connecticut, Kensett started work as an engraver in his father's and uncle's business. Over the next twelve years his work as an engraver took him to various cities in New York and Connecticut. In 1840, he left for England with Asher B Durand and John W Casilear. During his stay in England he studied English landscape painting. His travels then took him to France, Italy and Germany. On his return he traveled to the Adirondacks, the Berkshires and the Catskills.

He opened a studio in New York City in 1848 and the following year was elected to the National Academy of Design. His summers were spent on sketching tours in the New York and New England area and these sketches formed the basis of his paintings in the winter months in his New York studio. He extended his travels to the Mississippi area and to the American West, and revisited Europe but the source of most of his work remained the landscape of New York and New England.

EASTMAN JOHNSON 1824–1906

Born in Lovell, Maine, Johnson's early work consisted of portrait drawings of politicians. He trained at the Düsseldorf Academy in Germany in the company of several other distinguished American artists such as Albert Bierstadt and Worthington Whittredge. From Düsselfdorf he went on to study the work of the Dutch and Flemish painters in The Hague and he also spent some time working in Paris.

Returning to the USA he settled in Nantucket, Massachusetts,

ROCKWELL KENT 1882–1971

Born in Tarrytown Heights, New York, Kent was an architecture student at Columbia University and attended the summer art classes of William Merritt Chase. He became a full-time student at Chase's New York School of Art, where he came under the influence of Robert Henri and Kenneth Hayes Miller.

From 1904–13 he practiced as a draftsman for short periods, joined the Socialist Party, and married. In conjunction his life, though in his hands it preserved a solidity of form and a strength of outline.

As a member of the Eight he took part in the exhibition at the Macbeth Gallery which established them as the Ash Can School. He exhibited works in the Armory Show in New York, which he helped to organize.

GEORGE LUKS 1867–1933

Born in Williamsport, Pennsylvania. After attending the Pennsylvania Academy of Fine Arts in Philadelphia, Luks lived in Europe for ten years. On his return to the United States he became an artist/reporter for the *Philadelphia Press*. Here he met William Glackens, Everett Shinn and John Sloan and through them Robert Henri. He covered the Spanish American War in Cuba with William Glackens. After moving to New York he painted scenes of the city street life.

Luks exhibited with the Eight at the Macbeth Gallery in New York, after which they became known as the Ash Can School. In addition to city slum life he also painted mining scenes from his childhood in Pennsylvania.

STANTON MACDONALD-WRIGHT 1890–1973

Born in Charlottesville, Virginia, Wright visited France where he studied at the Ecole des Beaux Arts and the Académie Julian in Paris. He met Morgan Russell in Paris and they developed a style of painting which they called Synchromism. There are strong affinities in this style with that developed by Robert Delauney which is known as Orphism. Synchromism is based on the ideas of Cézanne which demonstrate how color can be used to describe space.

Wright returned to the United States and became disillusioned by the lack of interest in Modernism. He abandoned abstraction, and between 1935 and 1942 he directed the Federal Art Project of the Works Progress Administration in California and taught in Californian universities.

He traveled to Japan where he gave lectures about art and learned about the Japanese culture and language. On his return to the USA he resurrected his ideas on Synchromism and a retrospective of his paintings in the Los Angeles County Museum encouraged him to pursue his painting career again.

JOHN MARIN 1870–1953

Born in Rutherford, New Jersey, Marin studied at the Pennsylvania Academy of Fine Arts. His art studies continued at the Art Students League in New York. He moved to Europe and studied in Paris, coming into contact with Modernism. In 1909 he held his first one-man show at Stieglitz's 291 Gallery and became closely associated with Stieglitz after 1911. He also took part in the Armory Show in New York. His work at this time was inspired by the life of New York City, particularly by its skyscraper buildings and its lights.

Marin began to spend his summers on the coast of Maine which provided him with a source of material for his paintings. From the 1920s he used landscape as his major source of material, though the city still appeared in some paintings. In the 1930s he began to use oil paint, though it is his watercolors that are generally agreed to reveal his strengths.

Eastman Johnson

with Robert Henri he was instrumental in the organization of the Exhibition of Independent Artists.

Much of his work in the 1930s was in the form of illustrations for books, including his own travel journals. In 1967 he received the Lenin Peace Prize, part of which he gave to North Vietnam. His publications include *Wilderness – A Journal of Quiet Adventure in Alaska, Rockwellkentiana,* and *It's me, O Lord.*

FITZ HUGH LANE 1804–1865

Born in Gloucester, Massachusetts, Lane worked for various lithographic firms in Gloucester and Boston. He established his own lithographic business and returned to Gloucester where the primary sources of images for his paintings were. These paintings were reproduced by him as lithographs and sold by subscription. His mature style of painting, characterized by precise rendering of light and linear clarity, show Lane as one of the major exponents of the Luminist style.

ERNEST LAWSON 1873-1939

Born in San Francisco, California, Lawson was apprenticed to a salesman in Kansas City and learned textile design techniques. For a short time he studied at the Kansas City Art League School. In 1889 he went to Mexico City with his family where he studied at the San Carlos Academy and to New York to study at the Art Students League under J Alden Weir and JH Twachtman. In Paris he met Alfred Sisley. The Impressionist influences of Weir, Twachtman and Sisley confirmed Lawson as an Impressionist painter and he retained this style throughout

REGINALD MARSH 1898–1954

Born in Paris of American parents who were both artists, Marsh attended Yale University, then became an illustrator for *Harper's Bazaar* and the *New York Daily News*. He joined the *New Yorker* as a staff member in 1925 and went to Europe to study the paintings of Peter Paul Rubens, on which he began to base his style. Kenneth Hayes Miller encouraged him to paint the life of the city which produced some of his strongest works. His themes include Coney Island, The Bowery, Times Square and the squalor and shabbiness of city life.

THOMAS MORAN 1837–1926

Born in Bolton, Lancashire, England, Moran went to America with his family and settled in Philadelphia. He was first apprenticed to a wood engraver and then turned to painting with some instruction from a marine painter, James Hamilton. On a visit to England he was impressed by the work of JMW Turner and made studies from his paintings which were hung at that time in the National Gallery.

A second visit to Europe took him to England, France and Italy. When he returned to the US he joined Dr FV Hayden's expedition to the Yellowstone – a government-sponsored geological survey. His second visit to the West took him to the Rockies and the Grand Canyon of the Colorado River. From information gathered on these expeditions he produced his large canvases. These large canvases were important both as the first painted record of some of the territory visited by Western expeditions as well as being important paintings in their own right. On the expeditions two sites were named in honor of him – Mount Moran in the Teton Range, Wyoming, and Moran Point, Arizona.

SAMUEL FINLEY BREESE MORSE 1791–1872

Born in Charlestown, Massachusetts, Morse graduated from Yale University, then went to England with Washington Allston to study with Benjamin West at the Royal Academy, where he won the Gold Medal. He helped to form the National Academy of Design in New York and became its first president.

Much of his work consisted of portraits mainly because of financial pressures; in spite of his status he was never financially successful as an artist. His second trip to Europe included time in Rome with James Fenimore Cooper. On his return to the United States he began to spend more time on his scientific interests and especially the electromagnetic telegraph.

By 1937 he had completely abandoned his painting and concentrated exclusively on his inventions. A third visit to Europe brought him in contact with the daguerreotype and its inventor, Daguerre. Morse was intrigued by this new development in photography and became instrumental in introducing it to the United States.

GRANDMA MOSES 1860–1961

Born Anna Mary Robertson in Greenwich, New York, she married Thomas Salmon Moses at 17 and moved to a farm in

Grandma Moses

Virginia. Over the next 15 years ten children were born, five of whom died in infancy. In 1905 she moved with her family to a farm in Eagle Bridge in New York State and in 1927 her husband died. Her painting career dates from this time with work in local fairs and sales.

Louis J Caldor discovered her work in a drugstore in Hoosick Falls, New York, and the following year three of her paintings were included in an exhibition at the Museum of Modern Art. In 1940 her first solo show was held at the Galerie St Etienne, New York. From this point on she exhibited regularly in New York. Some of her paintings were published as Christmas cards, marking the beginning of a long-term relationship with Hallmark cards. On her hundredth birthday an exhibition of her paintings was held at the IBM Gallery in New York.

WILLIAM SIDNEY MOUNT 1807–1868

Born at Setauket, Long Island, New York, Mount was apprenticed to his brother, Henry Smith Mount, a sign painter in New York City. He then trained at the National Academy of Design, New York. His income derived primarily from portraiture, although his reputation now is based more on his 'genre' scenes and his landscapes. These date from the 1830s onwards and are taken from images of Long Island where he lived from 1836. His studies of European painting were not based on travel abroad but on reading and exhibitions in New York City.

His mature style of landscape is close to the Luminist painters of the nineteenth century in its concentration on exploring the various effects of light in detail.

GEORGIA O'KEEFFE 1887–1986

Born in Sun Prairie, Wisconsin, O'Keeffe studied at the Art Institute of Chicago. Her art studies were continued under William Merritt Chase at the Art Students League in New York City. She worked as a commercial artist in advertising in

Chicago, then attended the University of Virginia, Charlottesville. In subsequent years she was an instructor at the summer school at the University of Virginia.

Alfred Stieglitz first exhibited some of her abstract drawings in 1916, in his 291 Gallery in New York. She married Stieglitz in 1924. Her source of inspiration throughout her life was based on organic forms, flowers, bones and landscape. She traveled to Taos, New Mexico, with some friends, after which she moved to New Mexico and produced many paintings based on its landscape and the elements that made it up.

Her work from the 1940s was based on the enlargement of a single detail to form the whole painting and the image became more abstract. In 1945, she bought a house in New Mexico and settled there permanently after the death of Alfred Stieglitz. From 1953–69 she traveled extensively in Europe, Asia, India, the Middle East and North America. Major retrospective exhibitions of her work have been held in the United States, in Chicago, New York, Dallas and Worcester, Massachusetts.

JOSEPH PICKETT 1848–1918

Born in New Hope, Pennsylvania, Pickett's early life was spent as a carpenter, learning the craft from his father. After his marriage his interest began to focus on painting. A painting sent by Pickett to the annual exhibition in 1918 at the Pennsylvania Academy of Fine Arts received three jury votes, including that of Robert Henri. Only four paintings by Pickett are known to survive and it was only in the 1930s that his work really began to receive general recognition.

PAUL JACKSON POLLOCK 1912–1956

Born in Cody, Wyoming, Pollock went to New York City where he enrolled at the Art Students League and studied under Thomas Hart Benton. Pollock absorbed the Expressionist tendencies demonstrated by Benton and developed them further to create his own personal style.

During the 1930s he was employed by the Federal Art Project of the Works Progress Administration which allowed him to continue with his experiments. This was also the period when he met the Mexican muralists Rivera, Orozco and Siqueiros.

Works from the 1940s show many influences but Surrealism predominates and in 1947 the beginnings of his drip paintings, with their overtones of Surrealist automatic writing and with Oriental calligraphy, emerged. He abandoned color for black and white for several years in these large works and his work became more frenzied but in 1952 he turned once again to large colored works, which show him to be one of the major members of the Abstract Expressionist movement and a major American twentieth-century artist.

Jackson Pollock

Larry Rivers

MAURICE BRAZIL PRENDERGAST 1859–1924

Born at St John's, Newfoundland, Prendergast and his family moved to Boston while he was very young. After leaving school he became apprenticed to a commercial art business. He spent three years in Paris studying at the Académie Julian and the Atelier Colorossi. During the 1890s he exhibited in Boston, New York and in Philadelphia. Prendergast traveled to Italy and France and produced many watercolors based on what he saw there. During his visit he stayed for several months in Venice.

In 1905, he had a one-man show at the Macbeth Gallery and some time later Robert Henri invited him to exhibit in the controversial show of the Eight – the Ash Can School show – at the Macbeth Gallery. He also took part in the Armory Show in New York. His art owes much to European trends in the early twentieth century but using them as a basis, he developed a personal style which is considered to be the only American manifestation of post-Impressionism.

ROBERT RAUSCHENBERG 1925–

Born in Port Arthur, Texas, Rauschenberg studied at the Kansas City Art Institute and School of Design. He then went on to Paris to study at the Académie Julian, and then to Josef Albers at his Black Mountain College, North Carolina, where he met John Cage and Merce Cunningham. His next move was to New York City where he studied at the Art Students League.

His first one-man show was in New York at the Betty Parsons Gallery in 1932 and he began a long working relationship with Merce Cunningham and his dance company. Leo Castelli's acceptance of him for a one-man show established Rauschenberg as a major figure in the New York art world.

His paintings combine scrap material with traditional painted surfaces and form a link between the Abstract Expressionists and the Pop Art Movement. He has had retrospective exhibitions in New York, London, Minneapolis and Washington, DC, and his awards include the Grand Prize for Painting at the Venice Biennale in 1964.

LARRY RIVERS 1923–

Born Yitzroch Loiza Grossberg in the Bronx, New York, he changed his name to Larry Rivers on beginning a career as a jazz musician. He studied music at the Juilliard School of Music in New York and toured with the big bands.

On the advice of the painter Nell Blaine he enrolled in the Hans Hofmann School of Art in 1947 while continuing to support himself as a musician. In 1950 he traveled for a year to Europe where the work of Bonnard and Soutine impressed him. His work adopted the spontaneous brushwork typical of the Abstract Expressionists and combined it both with images from the commercial world and with ready-made images such as Old Masters' paintings.

In the 1960s his work expanded to include constructions, collages, prints and shaped canvases. In addition to the immense range of media in which he works, he has also taken part in films as an actor and has been involved in making videotapes. He has had numerous exhibitions.

THEODORE ROBINSON 1852–1896

Born in Irasburg, Vermont, Robinson moved with his family to Illinois and then to Wisconsin. He studied art in Chicago and at the National Academy of Design in New York. He also studied with Carolus-Duran and with Gérome in France. Returning to New York City he was elected in 1881 to the Society of American Artists. Robinson returned to France where he painted at Barbizon and over the rest of his life he made frequent trips between France and America. He became friends with Monet and stayed with him at Giverny.

MARK ROTHKO 1903–1970

Born in Dvinsk, Latvia, Rothko emigrated with his parents to the USA in 1913. He attended the Art Students League where he studied under Max Weber. Between 1936 and 1937 he was one of the many artists employed by the Federal Art Project of the Works Progress Administration. With Robert Motherwell, Barnett Newman and William Baziotes he founded an art school which became known as the Club. His work from the late

Mark Rothko

Ben Shahn

1940s shows an abandoning of the early influences of Surrealism and he gradually removed from his work references to form and figuration. Through a process of simplification he arrived at the diffuse rectangles which float against the surface of the canvas and allowed him to explore color relationships during the 1950s.

There are strong links in his painting with the contemplative elements of eastern religions and also the early American landscape painters who saw in their paintings a celebration and glorification of God's creations.

ALBERT PINKHAM RYDER 1847–1917

Born in New Bedford, Massachusetts, Ryder was largely self-taught but had some lessons from William E Marshall, a portrait painter. He studied briefly at the National Academy of Design in New York, and exhibited in its show in 1873. In the 1880s he turned from his early pastoral scenes to imaginary subjects and images from the Bible, Chaucer and Shakespeare.

His imagery has little relation to other painters and was intensely personal and though there are echoes of Turner in the structure of his paintings with their swirling shapes, they are closer to twentieth-century developments of Expressionism and Abstraction. Ten paintings of his were included in the Armory show though he produced very few new paintings after 1900.

BEN SHAHN 1898–1969

Born in Kovno, Lithuania, Shahn emigrated to the United States in 1906. To support himself while he completed his high school education in evening classes he worked as an apprentice lithographer. For a short time he attended the Art Students League in New York. He studied biology at City College in New York and also painting at the National Academy of Design. He also studied in Paris and traveled in Italy and Africa until 1927. After this his work showed a concern with social comment.

His first important paintings were a series based on the trial of Sacco and Vanzetti, the anarchists. He worked as an assistant to Diego Rivera on the murals for the Rockefeller Center, New York. He designed sets for the Jerome Robbins' ballet *New York Expert-Opus Jazz* and for e.e. cummings' *Him* and Jerome Robbins' *Events*.

CHARLES SHEELER 1883–1965

Born in Philadelphia, Sheeler studied at the Philadelphia School of Industrial Design, then trained under William Merritt Chase at the Pennsylvania Academy of Fine Arts, Philadelphia. In 1908 he traveled to England and stayed until 1909 in Italy and Paris where he came under the influence of Cubism. While continuing to paint, he worked as a commercial photographer.

He took part in the Armory Show of 1913 and exhibited with the Society of Independent Artists. He had his first exhibition of photographs at the Modern Gallery in New York, and settled in New York in this year. From around this time he began to use photographs to explore compositional ideas for his paintings.

During the 1930s and 1940s he painted rural images, though he retained his Precisionist style. By the late 1940s and 1950s he returned to industrial architecture and city scenes.

EVERETT SHINN 1876–1953

Born in Woodstown, New Jersey, Shinn studied at the Pennsylvania Academy of Fine Arts, Philadelphia, and while he worked as an illustrator for the *Philadelphia Press* he joined John Sloan, William Glackens and George Luks at the studio of Robert Henri to discuss art. He moved to New York where he joined the Eight under the leadership of Henri. In New York he worked for several magazines and also illustrated children's books. He exhibited with the Eight at the Macbeth Gallery in New York, where they became known as the Ash Can School.

JOHN SLOAN 1871–1951

Born in Lock Haven, Pennsylvania, Sloan trained at the Pennsylvania Academy of Fine Arts after which he worked as an artist/reporter for various newspapers. His first newspaper job was with the *Philadelphia Press* and he was employed by the *Philadelphia Enquirer*. During this period he came into contact with Robert Henri and was persuaded to take up painting as opposed to continuing solely with illustration.

He joined Henri in 1903 and, following his advice, painted while supporting himself by his newspaper work. He took part in the exhibition of the Eight at the Macbeth Gallery, where they acquired the name Ash Can School and he exhibited in the Independents Show arranged by Henri and Rockwell Kent. From 1911–16, he was art editor of *The Masses* but eventually felt compelled to resign because of his disagreement with its policy of social propaganda in art.

ROBERT SMITHSON 1938–1973

Born in Passaic, New Jersey, Smithson studied at the Art Students League, New York, with further studies at the Brooklyn Museum. He traveled to Rome and married artist Nancy Holt. From 1965 he started to visit quarries in the US and Canada, where he collected rock fragments which he arranged in heaps, developing his ideas of earth sculpture. These were often combined with maps and photographs. His interest in earthworks led him to England where he visited Stonehenge and other ancient structures. *Spiral Jetty* was executed in 1970 but the work is now submerged.

Clifford Still

JOHN MIX STANLEY 1814–1872

Born in Canandaigua, New York, Stanley was orphaned and apprenticed to a coachmaker. In search of a better job he moved to Detroit where he became a painter of houses and signs. James Bowman, a portait painter who had trained in Italy, gave him lessons. From 1836–8 he painted portraits around Chicago, and at Fort Snelling, Minnesota, he started painting Indians. After three years of portrait painting in the East he saved enough money to go West again to Fort Gibson, Oklahoma, where he painted Indian portraits and Indian scenes.

His collection of 150 paintings was put on display in the Smithsonian Museum in Washington, DC, when he offered it to the US government for $19,200 plus $12,000 in expenses. He became the official artist for another expedition, surveying for the railroad. From the numerous sketches he produced a vast panorama of forty-two scenes but this work is now lost. Congress did not accept the offer of his Indian Gallery and in 1865 it was destroyed by fire in the Smithsonian. Other works by him were also destroyed by fire in PT Barnum's Museum in New York.

JOSEPH STELLA 1877–1946

Born in Muro Lucano, near Naples, Italy, Stella came to the United States to study medicine and pharmacology. He changed his studies to art and attended the Art Students League and the New York School of Art in New York. He studied under William Merritt Chase and attended his summer school at Shinnecock in 1901 and 1902. His early involvement with the art world was as a magazine illustrator. He returned to Italy and also visited France. During this visit he came into contact with the Italian Futurists whose influence appears in his work from this time onwards.

He took part in the Armory Show in New York. His work took

its inspiration from the life of the city and especially from the image of the Brooklyn Bridge, depicted with fragmented shapes strongly reminiscent of the Futurists.

CLYFFORD STILL 1904–1980

Born in Grandin, North Dakota, Still moved with his family to Spokane, Washington. He studied at Spokane University then at Washington State University.

Still worked in the shipbuilding and aircraft industries during the Second World War and afterwards settled in New York where, with Rothko and others, he became one of the founders of Abstract Expressionism. From the 1940s he taught at various universities and colleges, including the California School of Fine Arts, Hunter College, and Brooklyn College. He has exhibited both in America and abroad and has received many awards.

JOHN TRUMBULL 1756–1843

Born in Lebanon, Connecticut, the son of Governor Jonathan Trumbull of Connecticut. During the American Revolution he served under Washington but following a dispute with the terms of his commission he resigned and returned to Lebanon to paint portraits and historical scenes. In 1780 he left for Europe and ended up in London in the studio of Benjamin West. His openly anti-British sentiments caused his arrest for treason and he was imprisoned until the middle of 1781.

He spent some time at the Royal Academy, where he painted several works with revolutionary themes. During the 1790s he served on various diplomatic missions in Europe for the American government. After the 1812 war he received a commission to produce four paintings commemorating the American Revolution and in the same year was elected president of the American Academy of Fine Arts, a post he held till 1836. In 1841, he published his *Autobiography*, the first autobiography written by an American artist.

JOHN HENRY TWACHTMAN 1853–1902

Born in Cincinnati, Ohio, Twachtman's first drawing classes were at the Ohio Mechanics Institute. He then attended the McMicken School of Design under Frank Duveneck. He continued his studies with Duveneck and traveled to Munich with him, where he studied at the Munich Academy until 1878, during which time he also visited Venice. He stayed in Paris and studied at the Académie Julian.

On his return to the United States his work developed along Impressionist lines. He settled in Greenwich, Connecticut, exhibited with Monet and J Alden Weir in New York and taught at the Art Students League and Cooper Union in New York. With Weir and Hassam he founded the Ten American Painters who pursued Impressionist aims in their painting.

JOHN VANDERLYN 1775–1852

Born in Kingston, New York. With the support of his wealthy patron, Aaron Burr, he went to Paris. He later produced sketches of Niagara Falls which he took with him to England for

His second visit to Europe was to buy paintings for American collectors. He taught at the Art Students League and Cooper Union in New York and exhibited at the American Art Galleries with Monet and Twachtman. In the same year Weir was a founder member of the Ten American Painters. From 1815–17 he served as president of the National Academy of Design.

THOMAS WORTHINGTON WHITTREDGE 1820–1910

Born in Springfield, Ohio, Whittredge started work as a house and sign painter with his brother-in-law in Cincinnati, and began to study art with Chester Harding. He trained as a daguerreotypist and established a business in Indianapolis. In the 1940s he exhibited his paintings in Cincinnati, and New York. He left for London and went on to settle in Düsseldorf until 1856; he was joined there by Albert Bierstadt then moved to Rome in the company of Bierstadt and Sanford Gifford.

He returned to the United States and was elected an academician of the National Academy of Design. With General John Pope, Whittredge visited the West, traveling to Colorado and New Mexico; a second journey to the West took place in the company of Kensett and Gifford. A visit to the Catskills, inspired by the paintings of Cole and Durand, encouraged him to paint his native country.

John Vanderlyn

engraving. His second visit to Europe was commissioned by the Academy of Arts of the City of New York to select material for its use. During this visit he stayed in Rome for two years and eight in Paris, and absorbed the current Neoclassical style.

On his return to New York he exhibited his *Palace and Gardens of Versailles* in panorama form. From this period until his death his work mainly consisted of portraits which were probably his best work.

MAX WEBER 1881–1961

Born in Bialystok in Russia, Weber came to the United States with his family at the age of ten. His first art education was at the Pratt Institute in New York. He then went on to study at the Académie Julian in Paris and later took lessons with Henri Matisse. On his return to the US he was taken into the circle of Alfred Stieglitz and exhibited at the 291 Gallery. At this time his work showed the influence of the Fauves and also Cubism. The Cubist-influenced works were generally replaced in the 1940s by a more Expressionist style.

JULIAN ALDEN WEIR 1852–1919

Born in West Point, New York, Weir studied art with his father and his brother John Ferguson Weir. He then went to New York to study at the National Academy of Design. In Paris he studied at the Ecole des Beaux Arts with Gérome. He traveled extensively in Brittany, Holland and Spain, where he admired the work of Velázquez. On his return to New York his painting reflected the style of Velázquez. In this year he was one of the founders of the Society of American Artists.

GRANT WOOD 1892–1942

Born in Anamosa, Iowa, Wood studied woodwork and metalwork in Minneapolis and opened a handicraft store in Cedar Rapids. His interest turned to art and he studied painting at the Art Institute in Chicago and in Paris, at the Académie Julian.

When Wood returned to Cedar Rapids his painting showed the influence of Impressionism. He was commissioned to produce a stained glass window for Cedar Rapids and went to Munich in 1928 to supervise its production. As a painter his first major success was *American Gothic* for which he was awarded a bronze medal by the Art Institute of Chicago. He was one of the leading figures of the Regionalist School of the 1930s, when he also supervised various projects for the Federal Arts Project of the Works Progress Administration and produced murals in Washington, DC, and at Ames, Iowa.

ANDREW WYETH 1917–

Born in Chadds Ford, Pennsylvania, Wyeth is one of the few artists in the twentieth century who has achieved fame and has remained in one place. He still lives in Chadds Ford where he was born and where he has spent all his life. He is the son of a well-known illustrator of children's books who taught him the basics of art. Other members of the family are also involved in the art business. His first one-man show was held in the Macbeth Gallery in 1937; he has continued to exhibit his paintings all over the world since.

His paintings are of landscapes and people of the American rural scene – he was first noticed for *Christina's World* (1948) – and this links him with the Regionalists of the 1930s. Like the work of his contemporary Edward Hopper, his paintings capture a sense of loneliness but Wyeth renders it with meticulous detail in watercolor and tempera.

INDEX

Page numbers in italics refer to illustrations.

ACKNOWLEDGMENTS

The publishers would like to thank the following individuals and organizations for their kind permission to reproduce the photographs in this book:

(The Metropolitan Musem of Art, New York has been abbreviated to: MET)

6–7 Worcester Art Museum, Massachusetts
8–9 Museum of Fine Arts, Boston, Bequest of Martha Karolik for the Karolik Collection of American Paintings
10–11 Museum of Fine Arts, Boston. Gift of William Sturgis Bigelow
12–13 Brooklyn Museum. Gift of the Brooklyn Institute of Arts and Sciences
14–15 Bridgeman Art Library/National Gallery of Art, Washington D.C.
16–17 National Museum of American Art, Smithsonian Institution. Museum Purchase
18BL Private Collection
18–19 MET. Gift of Mrs Russell Sage, 1908
21 MET. Gift of Samuel P. Avery, 1895
22 MET. Gift of Jonathan Sturges by his children, 1895
24–5 MET. Gift of Walter Knight Sturges, 1975
26–7 MET. Bequest of Maria DeWitt Jesup, 1914
28–9 MET. Gift of Thomas Kensett, 1874
30–1 Yale University Art Gallery, Gift of Arnold H. Nichols, B.A., 1920
32–3 MET. Purchase, Rogers and Fletcher Funds, Erving and Joyce Wolf Fund, Raymond J. Horowitz Gift, Bequest of Richard DeWolf Brixey, by exchange, and John Osgood and Elizabeth Amis Cameron Blanchard Memorial Fund, 1978
34–5 MET. Gift of Louise Floyd Wickham, in memory of her father, William H. Wickham, 1928
36–7 MET. Amelia B. Lazarus Fund, 1913
38–9 National Museum of American Art, Smithsonian Institution. Gift of John Gellatly
40–41 Bridgeman Art Library/New York Historical Society
42–43 Bridgeman Art Library/New York Historical Society
44–5 National Museum of American Art, Smithsonian Institution. Bequest of Helen Huntingdon Hull
46–7 MET. Rogers Fund, 1907
48–9 National Museum of American Art, Smithsonian Institution. Gift of Mrs Sarah Harrison
50–1 National Museum of American Art, Smithsonian Institution. Gift of the Misses Henry
52–3 Joslyn Art Museum, Omaha, Nebraska
54–5 National Museum of American Art, Smithsonian Institution. Bequest of Henry Ward Ranger through the National Academy of Design
56–7 MET. Morris K. Jesup Fund, 1933
58–9 MET. Bequest of Miss Adelaide Milton de Groot (1876–1967), 1967
60TL Yale University Art Gallery. Bequest of Stephen Carlton Clark, 1903. B.A.,
60–1 MET. Gift of George A. Hearn, 1910
62–3 MET. Purchase, Alfred N. Punnett Endowment Fund and George D. Pratt, Gift, 1934
64–5 Yale University Art Gallery. Bequest of Stephen Carlton Clark, B.A., 1903
66–7 Yale University Art Gallery. Bequest of Christian A. Zabriskie
68–9 National Museum of American Art, Smithsonian Institution. Gift of John Gellatly
70–1 National Museum of American Art, Smithsonian Institution. Gift of John Gellatly
72–3 National Museum of American Art, Smithsonian Institution. Gift of William T. Evans
74–5 MET. Bequest of Miss Adelaide Milton de Groot (1876–1967), 1967
76TL National Museum of American Art, Smithsonian Institution. Gift of William T. Evans
76–7 MET. Gift of Mrs John A. Rutherfurd, 1914
78 Brooklyn Museum, Dick S. Ramsay Fund
79 MET. Gift of Miss Ethlyn McKinney, 1943, in memory of her brother, Glen Ford McKinney
81 National Gallery of Art, Washington D.C., Chester Dale Collection
82–3 MET. George A. Hearn Fund, 1921
84–5 Whitney Museum of American Art, New York
86–7 MET. George A. Hearn Fund, 1921
88–9 Courtesy of: Hirschl & Adler Galleries, Inc., New York
90BL MET. George A. Hearn Fund, 1950
90–1 Corcoran Gallery of Art, Museum Purchase, Gallery Fund, 1916
92–3 National Gallery of Art, Washington D.C., Collection of Mr &

Mrs Paul Mellon
94–5 National Museum of American Art, Smithsonian Institution. Bequest of Henry Ward Ranger through the National Academy of Design
96–7 National Gallery of Art, Washington D.C. Gift of Edgar Williams and Bernice Chrysler Garbisch
98BL Museum of Modern Art, New York. Gift of Abby Aldrich Rockefeller
98–9 MET. Bequest of Miss Adelaide Milton de Groot (1876–1967), 1967
100–1 The Phillips Collection, Washington D.C.
102–3 MET. Arthur Hoppock Hearn Fund, 1950/© DACS 1987
104–5 Hirshhorn Museum and Sculpture Garden, Smithsonian Institution. Gift of Joseph H. Hirshhorn, 1966
106–7 MET. The Alfred Stieglitz Collection, 1949
108–9 Whitney Museum of American Art, New York
110–1 Hirshhorn Museum and Sculpture Garden, Smithsonian Institution. Gift of Joseph H. Hirshhorn, 1972
112–3 MET. The Alfred Stieglitz Collection, 1949
114–5 Whitney Museum of American Art, New York (Purchase 52.8)
115TR Newark Museum, Purchase 1937, Felix Fuld Bequest Fund
116–7 Whitney Museum of American Art, New York (Purchase 32.43)
118 Whitney Museum of American Art, New York
119 MET. George A. Hearn Fund, 1942
120BL The Phillips Collection. Washington D.C.
120–1 MET. The Alfred Stieglitz Collection, 1959
122–3 Corcoran Gallery of Art. Museum Purchase and exchange through a gift given in memory of Edith Gregor Halpert by the Halpert Foundation and William A. Clark Fund, 1981
125 MET. Arthur Hoppock Hearn Fund, 1932
126–7 MET. George A. Hearn Fund, 1942
129 MET. George A. Hearn Fund, 1943
130–1 Museum of Modern Art, New York, Abby Aldrich Rockefeller Fund
132–3 Whitney Museum of American Art, New York
134–5 Yale University Art Gallery. Bequest of Stephen Carlton Clark
136–7 Museum of Modern Art, New York, Purchase
138–9 Brooklyn Museum, anonymous gift
139CR National Museum of American Art, Smithsonian Institution
141 National Museum of American Art, Smithsonian Institution. Gift of S.C. Johnson & Son Inc.
142–3 Whitney Museum of American Art, New York
143 MET. Promised Gift of Renate Hofman
146–7 MET. George A. Hearn Fund, 1957
149 Whitney Museum of American Art, New York. Gift of Friends of Whitney Museum
150–1 Whitney Museum of American Art, New York
152–3 Whitney Museum of American Art, New York
154TL Gianfranco Gorgoni/Contact/Colorific!
154–5 © Christo 1976/photo Wolfgang Volz
155–6 Museum of Modern Art, New York. Gift of Mr & Mrs Robert C. Scull
158 National Portrait Gallery, Smithsonian Institution
159 National Portrait Gallery, Smithsonian Institution. Transfer from the National Museum of American Art; Gift of Miss May C. Kinney, Ernest C. Kinney & B. Wickes
160 © Wolfgang Volz 1985
161BL Hans Namuth 1987
161 Hans Namuth 1984
163 National Portrait Gallery, Smithsonian Institution. Gift of Ira Glackens
164 Hans Namuth 1987
165 Hans Namuth 1975
166 Hans Namuth 1980
167 National Portrait Gallery, Smithsonian Institution
168 Popperfoto
169 Hans Namuth 1987
170TL Hans Namuth 1970
170 Hans Namuth 1987
171 Hans Namuth 1987
172 Hans Namuth 1986
173 MET. Bequest of Ann S. Stephens in the name of her mother, Mrs Ann S. Stephens. 1918